BRITISH RAILWAY
LOCOMOTIVE
WORKS

D1386820

IN THE DAYS OF STEAM

An enthusiasts view
by
Bill Johnson

ACKNOWLEDGEMENTS

Compiling this volume of illustrations has been something of a pleasure, not just during those quiet moments alone when one could indulge in the nostalgia of the subjects illustrated but also when contact was made with like minded people. To share memories of those not so far off days and compare notes from countless 'number-crunching' expeditions, to all corners of the country, brought back happy memories which I hope will come over in this album. A lot of 'like minded people' have helped me to put together the captions to make them as informative and factual as possible. Others supplied photographs, usually at short notice, various documents and encouragement. To those people I would like to say thank you and they include A.B.Crompton, D.A.Dant, Richard Greenwood, Peter Groom, Ian G.Holt, R.C.Riley, Neville Stead, Alec Swain.
In particular I would like to convey special thanks to Willie Yeadon who made a lot of this possible and without whose help the project would probably not have completed. Les Peters came up trumps with some obscure requests for pictures from his post-war travels; Richard Casserley favoured me with many photographs of his late fathers taking. John Lees likewise supplied prints from his late fathers collection. Gordon Coltas burnt the midnight oil to ensure my requirements were met. Thanks gentlemen.

CHALLENGER
PUBLICATIONS

Copyright Challenger Publications 1995
ISBN 1 899624 04 X
Printed and bound by Amadeus Press, Huddersfield
First published in the UK by Challenger Publications
15 Lovers Lane, Grasscroft Oldham, OL4 4DP

INTRODUCTION

For those of you who ever visited a locomotive workshop in the days of steam, either officially or otherwise, this book will hopefully bring back many memories of the establishments how they used to be. Illustrated are the main yards, erecting and paint shops, scrapping facilities and some of those odd corners which held fascination for the curious. Railway enthusiasts, train spotters, number crunchers or just plain visitors - it didn't matter what title you claimed because we all went for one thing; to see the locomotives in all their glory. It did not matter if they were freshly painted or in pieces as long as we could see their numbers. Sometimes there was time to stand back and admire the giants but most of us just logged the engine numbers whilst others, thankfully, took their cameras and captured scenes on film which at the time was taken for granted because some of us thought, naively on reflection, that such things would always be with us.

Twelve workshops have been put into focus in this album and as you may realise many others have been left out i.e. Barry, Bow, Brighton, Caerphilly, Cowlairs, Gateshead, Highbridge, Inverness, Kilmarnock, Melton Constable, Newton Abbot, Oswestry, Rugby, Springhead, St Rollox, Worcester. Perhaps the aforementioned may form the basis of a second volume as space in this volume was at a premium to enable a good coverage to be given to each of the workshops.

In the main, most of the illustrations depict the BR period with some coverage of the post Grouping years and a couple of pre 1923 views, but all of them show scenes during the age of steam on our railways. Hopefully I have not offended anybody by leaving out their favourite Works equally I have tried not to give any particular establishment too much coverage though I have tended to gauge the size of the works with the number of views selected.

What has surprised me whilst compiling the material for this book, is the fact that most of the workshops no longer exist and those that do are but a shadow of what they used to be. There are many arguments about why our railway system is not what it used to be but the one fact that sticks out above all others is that we have lost a lot of heavy engineering capacity in this country and the expertise that went with it. To coin a well used phrase - "We may never see its like again".

BJ. Manchester 1995.

CONTENTS

ASHFORD

Opened in 1847 by the South Eastern Railway, Ashford works was extended after the SER had amalgamated with the London, Chatham & Dover Rly in 1899. Steam locomotive construction had been carried out since the earliest days and up to the amalgamation over 400 had been built there. When the old LC&DR locomotive works at Longhedge was closed in 1911 all locomotive building and repair of the new concern was centred on Ashford which between 1909 and 1912 underwent a massive extension programme more than doubling the size and capacity of the works. The nearby carriage and wagon works had undergone a similar enlargement shortly before the locomotive shops and the population of the town of Ashford grew apace with a New Town built specifically for the railway employees.

After Grouping the new Southern Railway did not carry out a wholesale renumbering of the 2,200 plus locomotives it had inherited from its three main constituents and instead allocated them to a section and a workshop broadly based on the old three company system prior to 1923. Ashford was charged with maintaining those locomotives allocated to the Eastern Section (the old South Eastern & Chatham) and up to 1931, when mass renumbering did take place and locomotives on that section had 1,000 added to their running numbers, a letter 'A' was painted above the number to denote that Ashford works was responsible for maintenance and consequently which 'section' the locomotive came from i.e. 'A' Ashford - Eastern, 'B' Brighton - Central, and 'E' Eastleigh - Western. That situation remained basically the same throughout the life of the Southern Railway and into the British Railways period up to the cessation of locomotive repairs at Ashford in 1962.

Ashford built diesel and electric locomotives for the Southern Railway from 1937, although not in any great numbers (three 350 h.p. diesel shunters Nos.S1 to S3 in 1937), a trend which continued until early BR days. Two notable diesel locomotives constructed for BR at Ashford were 10201 and 10202, the only main-line diesels built there. Emerging from the works in 1950 and 1951 respectively, the two huge 135 ton locomotives were equipped with English Electric 16CSVT engines rated at 1,760 h.p. each. By 1955 they were permanently allocated to the London Midland Region and were 'shopped' at Derby. During WW2 Ashford managed to build two main-line Co-Co electric locomotives, CC1 and CC2, for eventual use on the Newhaven boat trains and general freight work. Renumbered 20001 and 20002 by BR, they were joined by a third member of the class, 20003, built by Ashford in 1948. Other wartime construction included Q1 class 0-6-0's C17 to C36 in 1942 and in 1943-44 fourteen Stanier 8F2-8-0's, the latter part of an order for 130 locomotives built by the three Southern Railway workshops. Ashford was also responsible for cutting the frames of the West Country/Battle of Britain class Pacifics built by Brighton. The years 1949 to 1952 saw twenty six 350 h.p. EE engined 0-6-0 diesel-electric shunters constructed for the Southern Region, the last of these 15236 was the last locomotive built by Ashford.

The locomotive shops were remodelled after closure and incorporated into the adjacent wagon works complex with wagon building taking over from locomotive repair. Many of the BR Freightliner wagons were built here

Included (on pages 5-7) is a list of locomotives repaired at Ashford in 1954 and is typical of activities in the BR period.

(below) Home produced F1 no.1249 was being dismantled in the erecting shop on 26th May 1934 prior to a 'general' repair. Withdrawn some ten years later, the Stirling 4-4-0 had started life as one of 88 Class F passenger engines built by Ashford between 1883 and 1898. No.1249 had been built in 1897 and was rebuilt to F1 class in 1906 under Wainwright's instruction. H.C.Casserley.

On the same day another Ashford product, 1907 built E class 1176, resplendent in a fresh coat of paint, has some final adjustments made to the rear driving wheels before the locomotive is released to traffic. A test run prior to release has probably unearthed a problem which brought the engine back into shops for the wheel sets to be taken out. H.C.Casserley.

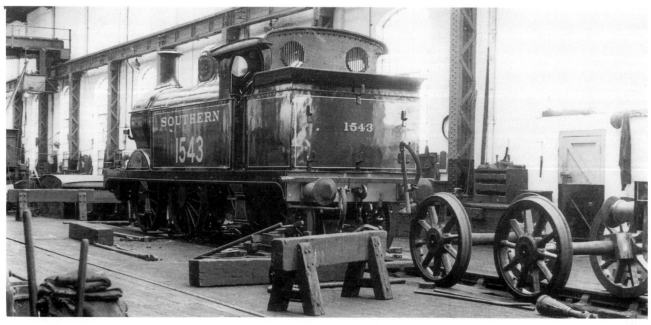

On 25th June 1939 Class H 0-4-4T no.1543 virtually sparkles in the early morning sunshine lighting the erecting shop. Fully lined out in its smart Southern livery (Brunswick green with black and white lining), the tank engine was amongst the last locomotives to enjoy this treatment before wartime brought about the austere unlined black livery of the early 1940's. This engine, yet another Ashford product, was fitted with push-pull gear in 1953 and was not withdrawn until 1962 aged 53 years. H.C.Casserley.

ASHFORD

Locomotives repaired in 1954.

Key:

1. Locomotive number.

2. Tender number (where two numbers are shown the first is the tender which arrived with the locomotive and the second is that which departed with the locomotive).

3. Type of repair i.e. G - General; H/C - Heavy Casual; H/I - Heavy Intermediate; L/C - Light Casual; N/C - Non-Classified; def - defect.

4. Date into works.

5. Date out of works.

6. Mileage since last General repair.

Note that locomotives are listed in order of departure after repair.

1	2	3	4	5	6
31777	677	L/C	24/12/53	5/1	39,413
31271	2918/2882	G	15/12/53	9/1	118,786
31749	654	G	16/12/53	9/1	128,044
31776	662	H/I	15/12/53	9/1	82,447
31404	3070	H/I	16/12/53	9/1	77,117
31258	2821	H/I	21/12/53	9/1	87,655
31229	2870	L/C	22/12/53	9/1	41,577
31239	—	L/C	22/12/53	9/1	38,930
31494	648	L/C	1/1	14/1	63,306
31402	3068	G	16/12/53	15/1	150,754
31519	—	G	18/12/53	15/1	156,473
32510	—	H/C	23/12/53	15/1	124,685
31280	2939	L/C	8/1	15/1	11,939
31272	2911	G	30/12/53	20/1	109,312
31174	—	G	1/1	20/1	77,419
31259	—	G	18/12/53	21/1	156,257
32442	2783/2790	G	1/1	23/1	134,843
31721	2913	H/I	31/12/53	23/1	63,272
31293	2958	H/I	7/1	23/1	90,840
33039	3178	H/C	11/1	23/1	25,700
32413	—	G	1/1	27/1	101,965
32456	—	G	31/12/53	28/1	72,942
32554	2790/2783	G	6/1	30/1	114,158
31793	1883	G	8/1	30/1	119,214
42106	—	L/C	4/1	30/1	100,670
31807	3053/3017	H/I	14/1	30/1	61,295
31867	3100	G	12/1	4/2	156,301
31767	667	G	8/1	5/2	87,444
42074	—	L/C	22/1	5/2	105,767
31828	3017/3053	G	15/1	6/2	124,535
31317	2955	G	15/1	6/2	165,975
31005	—	G	19/1	6/2	111,700
32508	—	H/I	20/1	6/2	133,993
32505	—	N/C	28/1	10/2	63,721
31259	—	def	5/2	10/2	47
31166	576/638	N/C	10/2	11/2	52,118
42096	—	L/C	29/1	11/2	100,716
31864	—	H/I	21/1	12/2	42,613
31909	1969/?	G	28/1	13/2	117,451
31065	2833	G	25/1	13/2	88,233
31865	1889	H/C	27/1	13/2	111,528
32522	2784	H/I	13/1	13/2	128,009
31894	1954/1969	G	29/1	20/2	151,640
31071	2888/2899	G	29/1	20/2	35,505
31495	2899/2876	G	4/2	20/2	131,783
31409	3082	H/I	26/1	20/2	48,075
31243	2905	H/I	29/1	20/2	61,566
32346	2989	L/C	22/1	20/2	37,652
31829	1882	L/C	1/2	20/2	109,602
31263	—	G	2/2	20/2	122,387
42070	—	L/C	11/2	25/2	115,453
30934	?	L/C	24/2	25/2	102,645
31549	574/608	G	9/2	27/2	100,996
31800	?	G	11/2	27/2	97,917
31843	?	G	5/2	27/2	161,515
32479	—	G	4/2	6/3	79,611
31690	2876/2888	H/I	15/2	6/3	69,983
31876	3101	G	9/2	6/3	133,157
31824	3033	G	12/2	6/3	119,385
32545	2876/2786	H/I	12/2	6/3	70,281
33021	3161	L/C	18/2	6/3	137,713
33036	3173	L/C	3/3	6/3	19,478
42105	—	L/C	19/2	6/3	115,476
31737	583/574	G	23/2	13/3	72,401
31866	3047/3057	?	?	?	?
31863	3057/3047	L/C	26/2	13/3	119,809
30801	?	G	20/1	13/3	135,007
31787	?	H/I	22/2	13/3	73,850
32460	—	H/I	18/2	13/3	61,221
31791	?	H/I	24/2	13/3	78,310
42099	—	L/C	26/2	13/3	125,194
31843	—	def	9/3	13/3	4
31720	2968	G	26/2	20/3	108,775
31633	1923	H/I	2/3	20/3	50,381
31244	2904	H/I	4/3	20/3	39,146
32441	2745	H/C	5/3	20/3	87,855
31523	—	G	5/3	20/3	?
32471	—	H/I	1/3	26/3	74,387
31737	574	def	23/3	26/3	nil
33020	3150	G	11/3	27/3	88,850
31627	3098	G	25/2	27/3	111,202
32534	2762	L/C	17/3	27/3	81,798
32557	—	G	26/1	27/3	82,416
32101	—	H/I	12/1	27/3	51,735
31059	2910	H/I	9/3	27/3	59,959
31263	—	L/C	22/3	27/3	373
32390	—	L/C	19/3	27/3	93,802
31628	3094	G	10/3	3/4	88,294
33024	3166	H/I	19/3	3/4	40,682
32459	—	G	17/2	3/4	125,622
32486	—	G	16/3	3/4	77,760
31548	—	H/I	12/3	3/4	62,102
30801	?	def	29/3	5/4	28
31325	—	G	12/3	8/4	52,347
32532	2771/2747	G	16/3	10/4	111,049
31223	2920/2909	G	24/3	10/4	139,102
31880	3105	G	18/3	10/4	109,170
31809	3091	G	23/3	10/4	107,995
32473	—	G	5/3	10/4	96,000
31370	2843	G	25/3	15/4	63,347
31852	3035	G	17/3	15/4	41,268
32170	—	L/I	26/3	15/4	49,696
80080	—	L/C	2/4	15/4	91,606
31714	2966	H/I	1/4	23/4	39,697
31759	688	L/I	2/4	23/4	44,656
30911	711	L/C	31/3	23/4	29,672
32487	—	G	10/3	23/4	124,306
31720	2968	N/C	26/4	29/4	595
31898	1958	L/C	13/4	29/4	139,451
31872	3064	G	6/4	30/4	131,981
31723	2975	G	8/4	30/4	89,127
31920	—	G	30/3	30/4	75,896
31905	3072	G	7/4	1/5	148,349
31757	686	H/I	9/4	1/5	86,604
31895	1967	L/C	14/4	1/5	31,179
31841	3039	H/C	15/4	1/5	121,472
32559	—	G	29/3	1/5	97,552
31904	1964	L/C	23/4	4/5	132,936
31018	2942/2920	H/I	15/4	8/5	79,370
31576	2944	G	14/4	8/5	96,959
31891	1951	G	15/4	8/5	156,350
31577	570	H/I	13/4	8/5	65,523
32347	2990	L/I	26/3	8/5	48,571
31413	3086	L/C	21/4	8/5	76,814
31542	—	H/I	13/4	8/5	60,070
32414	—	H/I	22/4	8/5	32,044
33006	3168	G	23/4	15/5	140,197
33027	3172	G	23/4	15/5	72,530
31768	2957	G	27/4	15/5	106,000
33022	3174	H/I	30/4	15/5	51,675
31278	—	G	11/2	15/5	76,172
31553	—	L/C	7/5	15/5	64,252
31666	—	L/C	3/5	15/5	96,109
31761	678	L/C	4/5	19/5	35,414
32523	2772	G	5/4	22/5	95,390
31719	2938	G	30/4	22/5	67,186
33037	3177	H/I	6/5	22/5	44,563
31634	1926	L/C	4/5	22/5	132,658
31184	—	G	28/4	22/5	58,867
31520	—	G	30/4	22/5	63,085
31925	—	H/C	5/5	22/5	13,509
32347	?	def	18/5	26/5	48,571
31925	—	def	27/5	28/5	13,509
31818	3000	G	11/5	29/5	161,182
31873	3062	G	20/4	29/5	157,749
31808	1898	L/I	13/5	29/5	61,753
31544	—	G	13/11/53	29/5	96,266
32497	—	G	7/5	29/5	104,421
32479	—	L/C	5/4	29/5	59
32570	—	L/C	14/5	29/5	62,420
31590	2894	L/C	28/5	1/6	140,762
33037	3177	def	2/6	3/6	44,563
33007	?	N/C	1/6	4/6	16,621
31295	—	H/I	31/3	5/6	63,273
31505	599	G	5/5	5/6	81,081
31781	681	H/I	14/5	5/6	107,595
33009	3162	H/I	20/5	5/6	90,702
31584	2903	H/I	21/5	5/6	37,149
31765	665	L/C	27/5	5/6	50,738
31717	2974	G	24/5	12/6	96,139
31794	1884	G	25/5	12/6	145,093
31802	3060	H/C	31/5	12/6	74,003
33018	3158	L/C	12/5	12/6	65,297
31870	3059	G	26/5	17/6	163,627

33001	3164	L/C	28/5	17/6	157,845
32340	2983	G	17/5	19/6	100,602
31890	3010	G	20/5	19/6	104,458
31033	2893	H/I	2/6	19/6	102,063
31227	2906	H/C	28/5	19/6	36,693
31714	2966	N/C	10/6	19/6	41,864
32562	—	G	31/5	19/6	105,297
31322	—	L/C	9/4	19/6	46,763
31808	1898	def	21/6	22/6	?
31716	2969	G	3/6	24/6	106,710
31771	671	L/C	23/6	24/6	156,684
31780	680	G	3/6	26/6	187,138
31893	1953	G	12/4	26/6	136,905
31784	691	G	4/6	26/6	87,495
31831	3031	H/I	14/6	26/6	71,859
31770	673	L/C	3/6	26/6	28,920
32458	—	G	10/6	3/7	76,504
31573	2954/2942	H/I	16/6	3/7	87,073
31862	3030	G	15/6	3/7	103,950
33012	3152	G	1/6	3/7	88,537
31796	1886	L/I	17/6	3/7	61,114
31910	1970	L/I	11/6	3/7	58,320
31807	3017	L/C	24/6	3/7	73,692
32352	2995	G	9/6	8/7	88,159
31585	2924/2954	G	9/6	10/7	134,139
31739	614	H/I	18/6	10/7	64,715
31611	3073	H/I	25/6	10/7	77,844
31823	3029	L/C	8/7	10/7	24,685
32494	—	G	23/6	10/7	83,643
31339	—	H/I	18/6	10/7	46,531
31619	1890	G	25/6	17/7	137,124
33038	3180	H/I	28/6	17/7	59,210
31865	1889	G	29/6	17/7	125,985
31815	3001	H/I	30/6	17/7	51,636
32337	2980	L/C	2/7	17/7	40,719
32408	—	G	22/6	17/7	94,614
32512	—	N/C	8/7	17/7	124,286
32352	?	def	14/7	17/7	88,159
31545	616/591	H/I	24/6	22/7	96,685
42069	—	N/C	20/7	22/7	121,725
31725	2923	G	6/7	24/7	121,425
32342	2985	L/C	6/7	24/7	81,040
31739	614	def	8/7	24/7	64,265
32109	—	G	2/7	24/7	115,525
31340	—	H/I	2/7	24/7	41,633
31319	—	H/I	7/7	24/7	40,691
32418	—	L/C	7/7	24/7	26,818
31704	—	G	8/7	24/7	109,270

31054	2945/2924	G	9/7	29/7	102,675
31267	2922/2945	H/I	13/7	31/7	65,292
31623	3099	L/I	12/7	31/7	129,650
31866	3057	L/I	15/7	31/7	58,522
31635	1925	H/I	15/7	31/7	62,813
31518	—	G	14/7	31/7	163,416
32351	?	G	1/7	31/7	86,758
33031	3159	L/C	16/7	4/8	30,783
33036	3173	N/C	23/7	6/8	28,151
31540	—	L/I	12/7	6/8	38,624
31780	680	L/C	16/7	7/8	528
31616	3066	G	20/7	7/8	140,736
32474	—	L/I	22/7	7/8	46,371
WORKS HOLIDAY 7/8 — 21/8					
31540	—	def	25/8	26/8	—
31588	2878/2922	G	22/7	27/8	96,725
31880	3105	L/C	4/8	27/8	9,396
31639	1929	L/C	28/7	28/8	39,601
31715	2977	G	23/7	28/8	110,790
31412	3084	L/C	27/7	28/8	32,487
31779	660	H/C	28/7	28/8	35,782
33014	3146	H/I	30/7	28/8	91,782
31892	1952	G	19/7	28/8	176,660
31825	1887/3050	L/C	25/8	4/9	101,251
31833	3022	G	4/8	4/9	187,740
31712	2964	G	23/8	4/9	89,152
31898	1958	H/I	5/8	4/9	146,972
31786	693	H/C	30/7	4/9	36,604
31164	—	G	26/7	4/9	146,639
31553	—	L/C	6/8	4/9	67,358
32351	?	def	12/8	4/9	144
31839	3008	H/I	24/8	9/9	67,297
31848	3050/1887	L/C	26/8	11/9	32,671
31861	3046	G	24/8	11/9	113,114
31788	695	G	26/8	11/9	121,408
31897	1757	H/I	1/9	11/9	51,688
31308	—	H/C	2/9	11/9	75,910
32338	2981	G	27/8	18/9	55,881
31763	675	G	27/8	18/9	154,120
33024	3166	N/C	7/9	18/9	51,710
31806	3075	L/C	9/9	18/9	206,363
31229	2870	L/C	7/9	18/9	55,130
31517	—	G	1/9	18/9	69,990
32577	—	G	3/8	18/9	90,315
31326	—	L/C	8/8	18/9	34,813
31899	?	N/C	7/9	23/9	42,782
31684	2880/2878	G	3/9	25/9	133,559
31682	2931/2880	G	13/9	25/9	116,773

Loco	No.	Repair	Date In	Date Out	Mileage
31743	617/616	H/I	31/8	25/9	91,230
31758	687	G	30/8	25/9	67,014
31625	1893	H/I	6/9	25/9	118,550
33028	3145	H/C	2/9	25/9	64,032
31842	3027	L/C	3/9	25/9	106,702
31593	2950	H/I	14/9	30/9	60,477
31847	3061	G	15/9	2/10	161,933
31086	2963	G	16/9	2/10	168,356
31832	3005	L/C	14/9	2/10	55,521
31404	3070	L/C	21/9	2/10	94,992
31918	—	G	9/9	2/10	102,407
31329	—	G	10/9	2/10	152,763
31898	?	N/C	29/9	2/10	149,154
32350	2993	L/C	22/9	7/10	89,828
31636	1924	G	21/9	9/10	174,854
31218	2951	G	27/9	9/10	118,860
31895	1967	H/I	17/9	9/10	45,183
31307	—	H/C	24/9	9/10	52,535
32351	?	def	9/9	12/10	—
31517	—	def	8/10	12/10	—
31901	1961	H/I	10/9	15/10	59,308
31191	2926	G	28/9	16/10	135,037
31509	589/617	G	20/9	16/10	143,623
32341	2984	L/I	23/9	16/10	51,928
31504	650	H/I	30/9	16/10	41,972
33005	3151	H/C	4/10	16/10	92,248
31523	—	G	23/9	16/10	212,164
31923	—	H/C	24/9	16/10	55,430
32500	—	H/C	29/9	16/10	24,570
33034	3144	H/C	7/10	22/10	37,162
31911	—	L/C	6/10	22/10	53,218
31615	3078	G	1/10	23/10	125,238
31879	3104	H/I	1/10	23/10	59,507
31400	3065	L/C	19/10	23/10	31,755
31265	—	G	30/9	23/10	114,950
32566	—	G	5/10	23/10	88,167
31894	1969	N/C	22/10	27/10	31,432
32535	2748/2771	G	6/10	30/10	108,787
31506	603/589	L/I	14/10	30/10	56,109
32547	2776/2748	H/I	12/10	30/10	56,360
31410	3083	H/I	15/10	30/10	65,244
31904	1964	G	12/10	30/10	143,101
32580	—	G	11/10	30/10	113,028
42096	—	N/C	15/10	30/10	129,865
31161	—	G	8/10	4/11	180,589
31068	2897	G	18/10	6/11	147,455
31061	2875	G	19/10	6/11	115,303
31896	1966	G	20/10	6/11	120,094
31903	1963	H/I	13/10	6/11	62,530
31863	3047	L/C	26/10	6/11	142,558
31107	—	H/I	15/10	6/11	43,195
31523	—	L/C	25/10	6/11	22,526
31492	602	H/I	21/10	11/11	114,009
31864	1897	L/C	28/10	11/11	73,153
32338	2981	N/C	5/11	11/11	1,923
31790	1880	G	26/10	13/11	190,494
31856	3024	G	27/10	13/11	142,492
31775	666	L/C	4/11	13/11	47,743
31246	609	L/C	29/10	13/11	27,718
31808	1898	N/C	5/11	13/11	76,636
31503	—	G	22/10	13/11	154,482
31489	613	G	20/10	16/11	146,594
31504	?	def	12/11	17/11	—
31900	1960	H/I	27/10	18/11	54,010
31686	2962	G	2/11	20/11	141,466
33012	3152	H/C	5/11	20/11	6,972
30903	703	N/C	16/11	20/11	8,807
32351	2994	N/C	12/11	20/11	1,525
32547	?	def	12/11	20/11	—
31919	—	L/I	4/11	22/11	48,886
33022	3174	L/C	4/11	22/11	64,329
31899	?	def	2/11	23/11	—
32165	—	G	28/10	24/11	128,033
31878	3103	G	3/11	25/11	177,101
33035	3149	L/I	8/11	25/11	55,701
31408	3081	G	10/11	26/11	152,881
31622	3097	L/I	11/11	26/11	59,651
31010	—	G	9/11	27/11	91,308
31500	—	L/C	11/11	27/11	69,724
31819	3036	H/I	12/11	30/11	40,822
33035	3149	def	29/11	30/11	—
31425	2839	G	10/11	1/12	107,426
31798	3092	L/C	17/11	1/12	48,819
31184	—	L/C	22/11	1/12	16,882
31871	3043	H/I	15/11	2/12	49,974
31239	—	H/I	19/11	8/12	74,385
31297	2931	H/I	23/11	9/12	64,649
32475	—	L/C	25/11	9/12	26,754
31145	645	G	17/11	10/12	95,112
31837	1888	G	25/11	11/12	168,177
31907	1955	H/I	16/11	11/12	134,929
31769	669	L/I	19/11	11/12	79,417
31915	—	H/I	23/11	11/12	48,161
31112	2892	G	26/11	14/12	94,107
31914	—	L/I	24/11	14/12	43,668
33029	3179	L/C	2/12	16/12	78,203
33030	3153	L/C	3/12	17/12	38,453
32480	—	G	26/11	17/12	88,589
32023	?	L/C	26/11	17/12	27,943
31898	?	def	8/12	17/12	156,099
31766	664/665	H/I	2/12	18/12	74,373
32166	—	G	30/11	18/12	86,150
31405	3071	L/I	3/12	22/12	174,525
31765	665/663	H/I	18/11	24/12	66,147
31846	3007	G	1/12	24/12	144,753
32451	??/2776	H/I	8/12	24/12	40,094
32547	2776/??	?	?	?	?
32343	2986	H/I	3/12	24/12	48,586
31875	3014	G	6/12	24/12	129,678
31812	3002	G	9/12	31/12	145,779
33032	3171	H/C	13/12	1/1/55	58,434
31319	—	L/C	21/12	5/1/55	55,280
31328	—	G	10/12	7/1/55	104,567
31764	?	G	10/12	7/1/55	139,372
31774	663/664	L/I	14/12	7/1/55	62,578
32581	—	H/I	14/12	7/1/55	44,107
31816	3006	G	10/12	11/1/55	92,269
31048	2806	N/C	22/12	11/1/55	77,860
31816	?	G	10/12	11/1/55	922
31857	3049	H/I	14/12	13/1/55	65,289
32410	—	G	7/12	14/1/55	90,358
31792	3003	H/I	20/12	14/1/55	88,672
31906	1965	G	21/12	17/1/55	107,210
31322	—	H/I	24/12	17/1/55	61,639
31922	—	G	15/12	18/1/55	72,658
31891	1951	N/C	22/12	18/1/55	18,787
31840	3045	H/I	31/12	20/1/55	68,770
31771	671	G	22/12	22/1/55	172,142
32491	—	G	29/12	24/1/55	67,030
32446	?	G	30/12	24/1/55	101,610
31785	?	L/I	31/12	25/2/55	47,532

Besides the repair of locomotives and their tenders, Ashford was also responsible for the repair of certain Departmental plant such as sludge tenders. Over the twelve month period of 1954, five Departmental tenders received various levels of repair as listed below.

Tender	Repair	Date In	Date Out
DS1325	G	23/4	4/5
737S	L/C	28/7	29/9
1211S	N/C	29/9	2/11
DS80	?	4/11	24/11
DS814	N/C	19/11	20/11

Ashford, like all the other BR Works, did its fair share of scrapping locomotives and in 1954 twelve were cut-up, all ex-Southern.

Loco	Class	Cut-up w/end
31703	R1	6/3
31038	C	27/3
31572	C	1/5
31660	R	8/5
31750	D	8/5
32588	E5	15/5
30282	T9	31/7
31729	D	7/8
31311	H	20/11
31493	D	25/12
31746	D	25/12
32487	E5	25/12

(opposite) On the site of the old locomotive running shed, closed in 1931, two U class engines, 31616 and 31791, wait in the yard alongside the Heavy Machine Shop. 31791 was about to enter the erecting shop (in the background) for repair and 31616 had just completed an intermediate repair during October 1961. In the following July all locomotive repairs ceased at Ashford ending 115 years of locomotive building and maintenance. R.S.Greenwood.

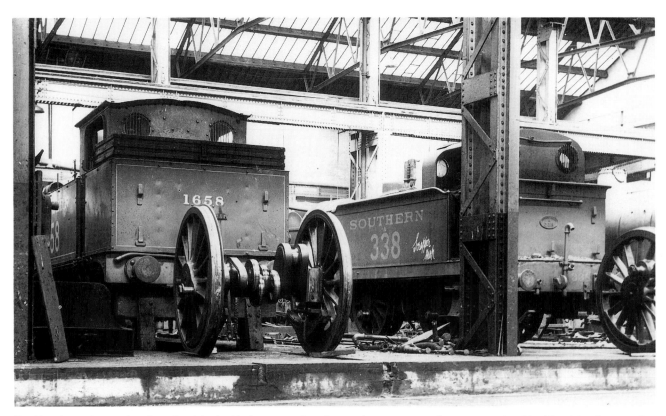

Besides the main erecting shop, furnished with three sets of tracks running east-west, there was on the side side of the shop another erecting shop with short stub pits served by a traverser which in turn was served by a turntable in the main shop. This was the old part of the works and when Ashford was building locomotives most were erected on these pits. In late May 1934 R class 0-4-4T 1658 is in for repair whilst R1 A338 has just been condemned as the legend 'scrapper shop' chalked on its tank proclaims. H.C.Casserley.

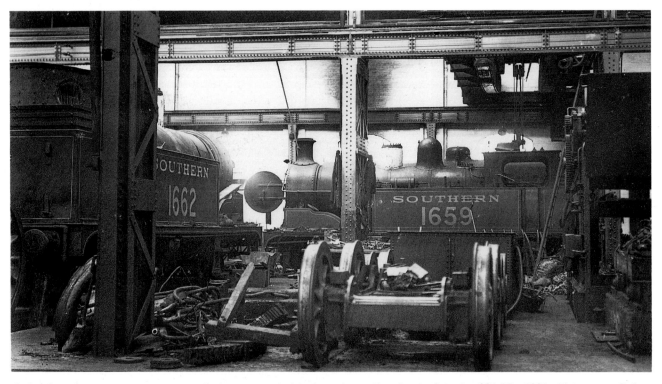

A view from the traverser avenue across the transverse pits into the main erecting shop on Saturday 26th May 1934 with two more R class members receiving attention. H.C.Casserley.

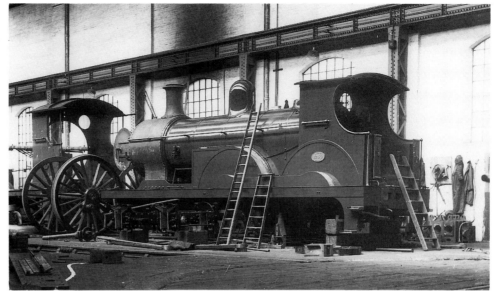

F1 4-4-0 No.1250 is in the first stages of its final repaint whilst still awaiting its wheels on the 26th May 1934. The boarded turntable, which turned engines for the traverser, is visible in the foreground. H.C.Casserley.

Before being married up to its tender U1 no.31890 has some final adjustments made for its return to traffic 29th June 1950. Black livery with red and white lining was now being applied as standard. L.R.Peters.

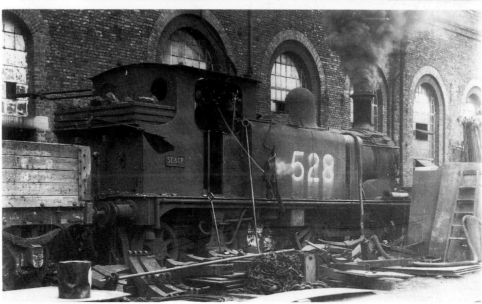

In late August 1927 ex-SECR A class 0-4-4T 528 was one of the stationery boilers employed by Ashford. Withdrawn in 1925, the engine was a Vulcan Foundry product of 1875 and built originally for the LC&DR. Still intact and complete with coupling rods in this view, it is unknown just how long it performed this duty until finally condemned. H.C.Casserley.

O1 class no.1378 has its last 'general' overhaul before the outbreak of war. The 0-6-0 is pictured in the erecting shop on the 25th June 1939 and is a Wainwright rebuild of a Stirling Class O. This particular shop was built in 1911, as part of the extensive additions to the locomotive works whilst at the same time the existing erecting shop, with its steam powered traverser, was extended. H.C.Casserley.

A view towards the east end of a very full main erecting shop in March 1956 with R1 No.31337 nearest the camera. H.C.Casserley.

CREWE

From humble beginnings Crewe locomotive works grew to become the largest such establishment of whichever company owned it. The LNWR built up the place, from the small complex sited within the junction at the north end of the station, until its western end reached out for one and a half miles from that junction. The LMS finished off much of the expansion scheme started by the LNWR and in 1926 introduced a 'belt system' where locomotive repair became a production line and at its height over 7,000 men were employed in its various shops and yards.

Such was the size of the place that the popular Sunday afternoon visits could take up to two hours if all the relevant shops were taken in and that usually meant at a continuous walking pace with no time to stop and admire the resident locomotives. Sometimes two or three parties could be seen being 'conducted' around the works with as many as fifty souls in each.

Right into the 1960's Crewe Works even had its own morning and evening workmen's trains which ran from Creswell right into the works yard. There was a signal box at the eastern end of the main works, near to the paint shop, to control the numerous comings and goings of the works shunters bringing stores and components, moving dead engines about and taking away the empty wagons.

Most of the former LMS 'standard' classes could be seen at Crewe and during the BR period many types of engines that were otherwise 'foreign' before 1948 came for repair or scrapping. The transition period from steam to diesel locomotive construction saw Crewe building types that would never return for 'shopping' because they were built for other Regions. A typical example being the 'Western' class C-C diesel hydraulics.

Whatever Crewe Works turned its hand to, it seemed that it was always on a bigger scale than any of the other BR workshops. There was always a large number of locomotives under construction at any one time besides the vast numbers in for repair. It certainly was a 'Mecca' and drew hordes of enthusiasts even after steam traction was banished.

(right) A visit on Sunday 14th August 1938 found this Webb 'Crane Shunter', no.3248, stabled near to the signal box at the east end of the main works. A large fleet of shunters were required at Crewe with up to twenty in use at critical periods. A.B.Crompton.

The twice, sometimes thrice, daily ritual of transporting 'dead' locomotives between Crewe South shed and Crewe Works and vice versa, could be seen right up to the end of steam repairs at Crewe. This 27th March 1926 view shows 'Super D' 2422 (later LMS 9301) hauling new 4F 4172 and ex 'general' repair and renumbered 'Super D's' 9278 and 9271 past Crewe North shed and by-passing the station en route to South shed where the ex-works engines would be prepared for a test run before being put into traffic. 2422 would have delivered a similar number of engines to the works for shopping before returning to South shed with this little cavalcade. H.C.Casserley.

Barely a year old, Princess Royal 6202 stands in the Erecting Shop in June 1936 receiving a 'light' repair, its third since being put into traffic. The Turbomotive retains its original domeless boiler but on another visit to Crewe less than a month later it received a new domed boiler. This locomotive, like most one-offs, did not fare too well during its life. Mileage and 'days out of traffic' figures suggest a problematic career which, as is well recorded, ended so violently at Harrow. Its lifetime mileage, including its last 11,443 miles as a reciprocating engine, was only 470,215 compared with sister engine 6203's one million miles plus in the same period although, 6202 was stored serviceable from 13th September 1939 to 19th July 1941! Authors collection.

Visitors inspect a line of Crosti 9F's being erected in April 1955. Crewe's capacity for building steam locomotives was enormous and as many as twenty could be at an advanced stage of construction in the erecting shops at any one time. L.R.Peters.

No. 10 Shop, the main erecting shop, in the early 1960's with mainly Stanier Class 5's and BR Standard types in for repair. Opened in 1926 as part of the massive enlargement of the building facilities and general reorganisation of Crewe Works, this shop contained three bays and each bay could accommodate about twelve of the largest locomotives on each of its two repair roads. Locofotos.

6100 ROYAL SCOT (alias 6152) in No. 10 Shop on 22nd July 1934 after completing its tour of Britain which commenced after return from its North American tour in December 1933. During its British tour the locomotive had worn the headlight fitted for the American visit but at this 'shopping' the headlight was removed though 6100 did retain the bell and the smokebox nameplate until sometime in WW2. W.L.Good.

An illustrious line-up of Stanier designs outside the Paint Shop in August 1950. Left to right are:- Class 5's 45341 and 44729, Jubilee 45721 IMPREGNABLE and 8F 48400. J.F.Thomas.

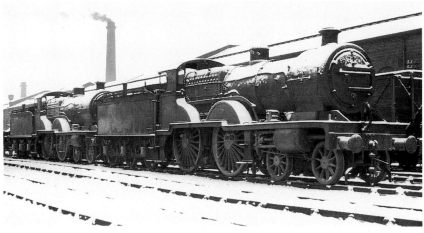

Ex Midland Compound's 41019 and 41041, each coupled to a condemned tender, await cutting up on a bleak 27th January 1952. Authors collection.

Western Region pannier 2111, from Carmarthen shed, was one of a number of ex-GWR 0-6-0PT overhauled at Crewe in early BR days. Because there were no spare boilers available at Crewe, each of the pannier's had to spend longer than usual in shops whilst their boilers were repaired. Sandwiched between an 8F and Royal Scot 46117 outside the Erecting Shop (No.10) in February 1949, 2111 was virtually ready to return to South Wales. W.L.Good.

CREWE 4th January 1953 Locomotives in the works for repair or otherwise.

LOCO	SHED	REPAIR
YARDS AND PAINT SHOP		
42121	1C	INT
42231	33A	INT
42253	33A	INT
42282	26A	GEN
42285	26A	GEN
42538	3C	GEN
42567	5D	GEN
42668	5D	GEN
42670	5D	DAM
44659	21A	INT
44754	20A	N/C
44775	20A	GEN
44838	1A	INT
44840	5B	GEN
44938	9E	N/C
44963	17A	N/C
45061	24B	INT
45148	5B	GEN
45284	26G	INT
45299	12A	N/C
45544	5A	GEN
45596	8A	DAM
46210	5A	GEN
46249	1B	GEN
46255	5A	GEN
46727	11B	CUT-UP
48613	9G	GEN
48658	1A	CAS
48757	2A	INT
48767	3A	DAM
49288	10E	DAM
58427	9B	N/C
58919	4D	CUT-UP
70011	32A	N/C
90269	38D	N/C
90283	24B	INT
90504	38E	GEN
90626	26D	GEN
WORKS SHUNTERS		
47592	—	—
49140	—	—
56032	—	—
58321	—	—
58323	—	—
58326	—	—
58332	—	—
58336	—	—
58343	—	—
58347	—	—
ERECTING SHOP		
41249	14B	INT
41274	20C	INT
42053	21A	INT
42134	14B	INT
42449	5D	INT
42543	5D	N/C
42555	24B	GEN
42560	10C	INT
42601	11A	DAM
42642	27D	GEN
42647	26B	GEN
44658	14B	GEN
44694	25F	INT
44695	25F	INT
44711	2A	GEN
44732	24E	INT
44747	22A	GEN

44769	8A	N/C
44817	14B	INT
44839	22C	GEN
44852	21A	INT
44869	2B	INT
44950	24E	INT
45039	8A	N/C
45102	26A	GEN
45142	10C	N/C
45193	11A	N/C
45197	12A	N/C
45329	10C	N/C
45415	27C	INT
45515	8A	INT
45552	12B	INT
45560	16A	GEN
45573	20A	INT
45604	5A	INT
45699	22A	INT
45725	19B	DAM
45735	1B	INT
45742	3B	GEN
46100	1B	N/C
46110	5A	GEN
46247	1B	INT
46252	5A	INT
46435	27A	INT
48188	8B	GEN
48449	2D	INT
49057	9D	GEN
49179	8D	GEN
49130	11A	GEN
49342	8D	CAS
49431	2A	GEN
70038	NEW	—
70039	NEW	—
70040	NEW	—
72001	66A	CAS
72006	68A	CAS
90073	38A	INT
90322	25G	INT
90342	25A	INT
90520	38E	GEN
90541	24C	INT
90633	24B	CAS
90679	25A	CAS

Total: **112**

Key:

CAS - Casual repair.
DAM - Damage repair.
GEN - General repair.
INT - Intermediate repair.
N/C - Non-Classified.

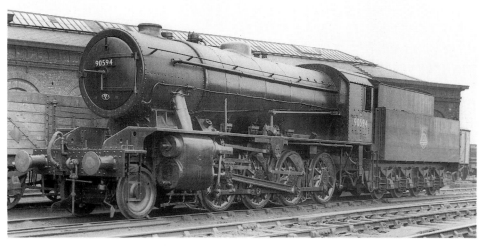

After repair, Eastern Region WD 'Austerity' 90594, from Colwick, waits beside the old works for its tow to South shed. W.L.Good.

At the east end of the main works complex, on the opposite side of the Chester line, stood the carriage storage sheds which were once part of the Carriage Works. In June 1948, with carriages long departed, the sheds were utilised to store Stanier 8F 2-8-0's (amongst other things) which had returned to the UK from service overseas with the War Department. Of the three engines visible, only those near the camera are identifiable as 70395 (later 48257) and 41-225. It was to be more than a year later before 70395 was moved into the works for overhaul and eventual return to traffic with B.R.. W.L.Good.

6133 VULCAN (later renamed THE GREEN HOWARDS) inside the Paint Shop in 1931. The northlight roof of this shop afforded a 'no-glare' natural light situation for the painters, however today we would regard the gas lighting as hardly conducive to proper working conditions. Locofotos.

All the LMS Garratts were 'shopped' at Crewe. On the 7th May 1939, after a non classified repair 7973 stands on the stabling roads having its number touched-up prior to being returned to the Midland Division. The erecting shop fitters did not take to the Garratts but as was their lot for twenty odd years they still had to repair them. Just lifting the boiler unit from the engine units entailed the following sequence of operation so it is easy to appreciate the dislike of the Crewe erecting shop personnel for these engines: (1) Water tanks must be emptied before equilibrium pipe wing nuts are uncoupled; (2) Uncouple vacuum hose bags; (3) Uncouple steam sanding pipe unions; (4) Remove pivot centre keeps - two to each pivot, one on the R.H. side and one on the L.H. side, secured by 2" dia. pins and split pins; (5) Remove steam pipes with ball socket joints. The ball sockets are released by taking out the set screw (secured by locking plate and pin) in the top pivot centre casting; (6) Remove exhaust pipes; (7) Uncouple flexible steam pipe unions; (8) Remove brake pull rods; (9) Remove short reversing rods. Pins over centres are beneath trap doors in platform; (10) Remove cylinder drain cocks pull rods; (11) Remove coal chute, cab roof, footsteps; (12) Pack up lifting bolts (normally these lie flush in platform each side of pivot centres; (13) Remove trap doors in wood platform in cab; (14) Lift boiler unit by means of lifting bolts at front end and hooks passed through trap doors in cab floor under main frame at rear end; (15) At about 5" lift release top pivot centres and the rear engine unit may then be drawn clear, after which increase lift to about 7" in order that the inner driving wheel may clear the top pivot centre casting. *All but one of these huge engines were eventually cut-up at Crewe, the odd-man-out no.47985 was dealt with at Derby Works in June 1955, whilst en route to Crewe, because industrial action had prevented its last journey being no further than Derby.* W.L.Good.

Another new Crewe product. Britannia 70006 ROBERT BURNS stands on Crewe North shed on 15th April 1951 before leaving for the Eastern Region and a glorious though short career hauling express trains on former Great Eastern lines. It was another Britannia, 70013 OLIVER CROMWELL, which became the last steam locomotive to be overhauled at Crewe, departing with due ceremony on the 2nd February 1967. W.L.Good.

BR-Sulzer Type 2 diesel (later class 24) D5061 needs only its bogies before delivery to the Eastern Region. This February 1960 view, inside the south bay of No.10 Shop, shows new construction going on alongside steam locomotive repair. Just over a year previously Crewe had built its final steam locomotive in the shape of BR 9F 92250 and with its departure a start was made on Crewe's first main-line diesel locomotives - Type 2 Bo-Bo's D5030 to D5065 and D5076 to D5093. Once these were completed the Erecting Shop turned its attention to a batch of BR-Sulzer Type 4's of which the first one D68 is just visible on the right. In the left background Fairburn 2-6-4T 42298 undergoes a 'general'. Authors collection.

The south bay of No.10 Shop in November 1960 with BR-Sulzer Type 4's D80 to D84 and D86 to D88 in varying stages of erection. The construction of diesel locomotives brought an air of tidiness to this area of the erecting shop, witness the demarcation lines and litter bins which was understandable because the 'new technology' required a clean environment during building if all was to go well. There had been some delay in construction of these diesels due to late delivery of parts from outside contractors but once those parts had arrived Crewe was turning out these 138 ton monsters at the rate of six a month. Later diesel classes built in part by Crewe included the 'Western' class C-C diesel-hydraulics for the WR and 200 Brush Type 4 which later became Class 47. British Railways.

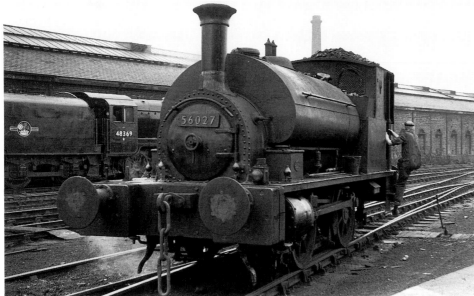

The Crewe Works shunting engines up to Nationalisation were mainly drawn from the ranks of former LNWR classes but as these were whittled down by withdrawals the fleet became more varied and engines from some unusual sources were seen working the different pilot turns. LMS Jinty 47505 on W6 with LMS 4F 44405 behind on W13, in November 1964 were not so unusual but in the earlier BR period ex-L&Y and ex-CR types were used and 'Pug' 56027 seen shunting on the engine stabling roads on Saturday 22nd August 1959 though not the first of its type to work Crewe Works pilots was typical of the interlopers. both A.Swain.

Former LNWR 'Special Tank' CD7 and 0-6-2T 58926 outside the Brass Shop on 8th November 1959. Both engines had recently been withdrawn, the latter for preservation. A.Swain

DARLINGTON

Opened in 1863 by the Stockton & Darlington Railway, Darlington eventually became the main locomotive manufacturing and repair workshops of the North Eastern Railway. After Grouping in 1923 the work did not let up and the place continued to expand. By the mid 1950's over 3,800 were employed, the highest ever. It was during the late 1950's that the variety of locomotive classes repaired at Darlington became more interesting and visits during that period always held the odd surprise for the enthusiast. During the LNER period most of the pre-Group types kept to the old company boundaries and hence repairs were carried out at the old company workshops. Darlington was no exception to this rule and former North Eastern locomotives would be repaired at Darlington or Gateshead, the other former NER works. So predictability was the norm until British Railways came into being and then it was to be some time before 'foreign types' started to arrive for repair. As other BR workshops contracted or closed in the early 1960's, Darlington began to take on more diverse classes; London Midland 0-6-0 tank and tender engines; Stanier Class 5 and Class 8F's, even 'Jubilee' 4-6-0's. Locomotive building under BR was no less interesting. To start off on a high note, Darlington built its first Pacific's for twenty five years and was responsible for twenty three of the forty nine highly successful Peppercorn A1 class; ex LMS designs then emerged in the shape of Ivatt's 4-6-0 and 2-6-0 mixed traffic engines; BR Standard 2-6-0's and 2-6-2T. In 1952 the first of many diesel shunters was completed and in 1960 Type 2 Bo-Bo main line diesel locomotives came off the production line and were to continue to do so until August 1964 when the last one, D7597, marked the end of locomotive building at Darlington. The last steam locomotive built was BR Standard Class 2 No.84029 in June 1957 for the Southern Region. Run-down to closure started in mid 1965 and the last locomotive to enter for a repair, in March 1966, was BR Standard 76040 which needed minor work on the superheater header but that was not carried out and within less than 48 hours the engine was sent to Darlington shed condemned. On 2nd April 1966, after 103 years of locomotive production and repair, Darlington Works closed for good. The last remnants of the locomotive works did not disappear until the summer of 1981 when the building that had once been the main erecting shop was demolished, its site now a supermarket.

(below) Darlington Works yard 1960. We are looking in an easterly direction, from the footbridge on Whessoe Road, at the main manufacturing shops of the works. Left to right they were; new engine shop; frame shop; axle box shop and, with chimneys and ventilators, the brass foundry. Behind these shops going back to North Road was the milling shop; cylinder and valve shop; coppersmiths; smithy and spring shops. The main erecting shop was just out of picture to the left as was the machine shop. The building in the centre of the yard was once a weigh house but by 1960 it had become a store. Like most locomotive works yards, Darlington looked something of a mess but there was a semblance of order which was not readily apparent to the visitor. Up to 1933, on the area just to the right of the old weigh house, a true roundhouse locomotive shed stood; disused for running purposes, after 1903 it was used for storing locomotives until demolished. Locomotives on view are mainly of LNER origin though there are a few boilers with Belpaire fireboxes which are probably of either BR Standard or LMS Ivatt Mogul origin. N.E.Stead

The east end of the erecting shop in 1957 with tender repairs taking up the bays. Locomotives, some of which can be seen in the distance, were repaired at the west end during this period. Locomotive access to the erecting shop, after they had been separated from any tender, was via a door in the west wall, onto a 50 foot turntable located in the centre bay, which turned them so that they were facing in a northerly direction and parallel to the repair roads. They were then moved backwards, forwards or left where they were on the turntable to be lifted by two overhead cranes and slung onto a vacant repair road; depending on which of the three bays of the erecting shop any loco was designated, influenced its movement off the turntable. Notice the shoring of the wall buttresses brought about by subsidence. British Railways.

Q6 63395 undergoes a 'heavy intermediate' repair in September 1965, last but one of its class to get one (63387 had a 'casual heavy' in the following November. The class had been associated with Darlington since 1913 and over half were built there between 1913 and 1919. No.63395 along with 63344 were the last Q6 0-8-0's in service, both withdrawn in September 1967. Purchased for preservation, 63395 now runs on the North Yorkshire Moors Railway. P.B.Booth per N.E.Stead collection.

- 20 -

A September 1950 photograph of another Darlington product, motor-fitted G5 67305 repainted after completing a 'general'. The engine is stood at the rear of the Weigh House and will probably be weighed first thing Monday morning assuming this is a weekend photograph. Out of a class of 110, only 21 were fitted for push-pull working and 67305 as No.1755 gained the P&P gear in 1941. Along with what others remained of the G5 Class, 67305 was withdrawn from service in December 1958 and was cut-up, appropriately at Darlington. The west wall of the Erecting Shop forms the backdrop for this superb portrait. N.E.Stead.

BR diesel-electric 0-6-0 shunter 12125 was amongst the first batch of diesels built by Darlington in 1952. A total of 385 of these and their successors the Class 08 DE shunters were built at the works. 12125 went first to Kings Cross shed and four years later to Stratford; a move to Immingham in November 1958 saw it end its days there in 1969. Authors collection.

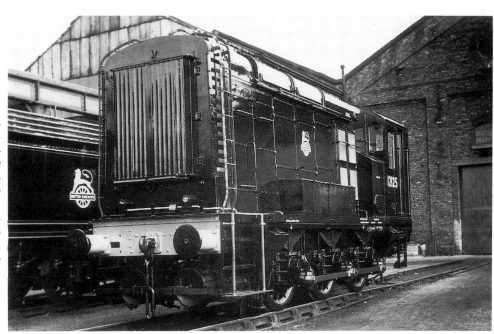

Another 1952 built locomotive was this Ivatt Class 2MT one of thirty-eight (46465 - 46502) such engines built for BR during 1951 and 5?. This one left the works in the January and was sent to Kettering, all the batch up to 46502 going to the London Midland Region. A lot the first batch, 46470 - 46482 stayed in the North Eastern Region and were 'shopped' at Darlington. National Railway Museum.

A8 No.69884 in the works yard 9th November 1958 having just been condemned, its re-usable shed plate has been removed but the smokebox number plate will go to the scrap yard with it, unless somebody bought - or pinched it. P.B.Booth per N.E.Stead collection.

The Works Shunters during most of the BR period consisted a batch of three or four J94 0-6-0 saddletanks and J94 68007 rests for the weekend on the Weigh House road, alongside the steaming shed on 29th September 1962. In the left background can be seen the Boiler Park gantry and the engine washing pad; in front of the Stripping Shop a WD 2-8-0 waits to enter. A.J.Cocker.

Unusual visitors in 1965 included Stanier 8F 2-8-0 No.48519, seen here on 30th January alongside the entrance to the Erecting Shop. Locofotos.

Class 4 BR Standard 75009, outside the Weigh House, was another stranger during that bleak January in 1965. To the right is the Steaming Shed. Locofotos.

J21 65033 was a long time resident of the Works yard at Darlington being withdrawn in April 1962 and finally sold in 1966 as the works was about to close. Together with sister engine 65099, which was withdrawn in October 1961 and resided in the yard until February 1966 when it was cut-up, the two locomotives or to be more correct parts from the two locomotives were to be assembled as one for preservation. These two views of the engines as they were in September 1965 shows the condition of each. Interestingly 65033 had escaped the breakers torch once before in November 1939 when, as LNER 876 it was condemned but because of foreseeable wartime shortages a repair was carried out and it was returned to traffic. both Alec Swain.

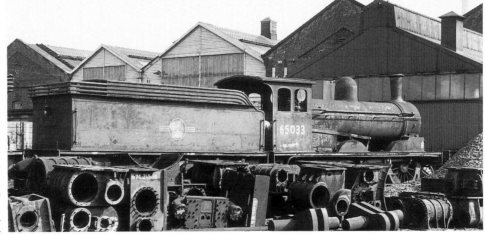

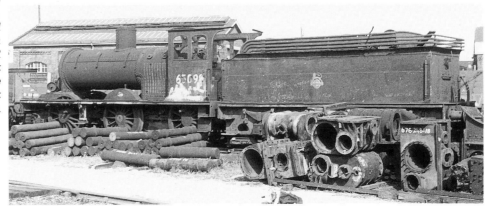

The main Erecting Shop from the works yard in March 1946. The sliding doors marked the only entrance/exit for locomotives; once inside engines were turned on a turntable and moved to a repair bay via overhead cranes. On the left of the picture is the Weigh House and on the right with its own overhead crane is the Tyre Park. Only two locomotives are identifiable by number, 5742 in the group on the left and 9868 standing on the dead-end road by the erecting shop doors. W.B.Yeadon collection.

An undated 1930's photograph inside the New Engine Building shop with D49/2 no.336 in for repair alongside an unidentified stripped down Sentinel railcar. Frames for new locomotives can be seen on the trestles to the left. W.B.Yeadon collection.

J71 no.68236 was one of the Darlington pilot engines in April 1953 and is dwarfed by its charge, L1 no.67746, outside the Weigh House. L.R.Peters.

Having just completed a 'general', this B1 is made ready to return its home shed at Neville Hill in April 1953. L.R.Peters collection.

North Road scrap yard held, only for short periods, more surprises than the main works over the years. Former Great Central, Great Eastern and Great Northern locomotives were dealt with as well as home built NER examples. The Darlington men were indeed efficient and ruthless. All except one of the fifteen Q7's were scrapped here (the sole survivor being 901 on the NYMR) and fifty one of the more numerous Q6 Class; in fact the list of ex-NER engines disposed of at Darlington is enormous. Locos of LNER and BR origin include two A4's, nine A3's, four BR Clan's, ten WD 2-10-0's; variety and numbers combined to make it an interesting place. Other oddities to be found there in the 1960's included the grounded bodies of Sentinel Y1 68149 and Y3 68180 in use as tool stores. Alec Swain.

(left) In the transition period from Grouping to Nationalisation both Doncaster and Stratford sent large numbers of withdrawn locomotives to Darlington for cut-up and J15 no.5380, withdrawn January 1948, was another of the Stratford lot sent in early 1948 and just missed out on a 60th birthday being cut up in April. N.E.Stead.

(opposite bottom) Of the six S1 Class 0-8-4T all were cut-up at Darlington in 1956/57 except 69903 which became one of Doncaster's victims after its withdrawal in March 1954. In 1957 and after a period of fifty years, ex-booster fitted 69901, built for the GCR in 1907 by Beyer Peacock, is being reduced to a pile of scrap metal. N.E.Stead collection.

(left) F3 no.7137 was withdrawn at Stratford shed in November 1947 and then journeyed north to Darlington for cutting up. Built by the Great Eastern in 1895, the Holden designed 2-4-2T is seen at North Road scrapyard in early 1948. N.E.Stead.

Darlington scrapyard, surrounded by large well established trees, had the surreal appearance of a graveyard and certainly the air of one. Another ex-GER engine, J69 no.68559, stands on the North Road site awaiting the cutters torch in the summer of 1956. E.Haigh collection.

(below) A8's withdrawn in June 1960 join the statistics at North Road scrapyard in July of that year. Note the different bunker tops. N.E.Stead collection.

- 27 -

DERBY

Derby like most other locomotive works had a long lineage being established by the North Midland Railway in 1840 and becoming Midland Railway property in 1844. The first locomotives built appeared in 1851 and by the 1880's Derby had become the main locomotive, carriage and wagon building and repair centre of the MR.

The Midland Railway had a number of 'outstation shops' at certain engine sheds strategically placed throughout the system where all types of repairs could be carried out on its locomotive fleet. Having a fleet renowned for its 'small engines', the MR could easily accomodate any engine within those fitting shops. However after Grouping and with the advent of larger engines the fitting shops gradually fell into disuse being neither equipped with the appropriate cranage and/or having no means of access other than by small turntables suitable only for the former MR types.

Derby now, along with the other main works on the LMS, came into its own and all 'heavy' repairs were concentrated on the main works. A reorganisation of the main LMS workshops in the late 1920's saw new practices introduced and old ones thrown out to create a greater repair capacity where locomotives spent less time 'in shops' and more time earning revenue.

Derby continued to build new locomotives for the LMS but now larger 'standard' types were emerging from the erecting shops. The first LMS diesel locomotives were erected at Derby, setting a precedence that saw hundreds more turned out during the 1950's and 60's for British Railways. The start of the BR period saw 'foreign' types appearing in the shape of Western Region 'Pannier' tanks and Eastern Region J39 0-6-0's, all in need of urgent repair.

Steam locomotive construction carried on until 1957 when BR Standard Class 5 No.73154 emerged as the last one from Derby. Steam repair was still in full swing in 1960 but not for much longer as Derby prepared to become the first London Midland workshop to concentrate on diesel repair. By September 1963 the preparations were complete as the last 'official' steam locomotive repair was completed to another BR Standard, No.75042. BR Class 9F 2-10-0 No.92102 slipped in and out of the works in 1964 for damage repairs becoming the unofficial but actual last one.

In just over a hundred years Derby had produced nearly 3,000 steam locomotives and in the thirty year period up to 1967 had produced a thousand diesel locomotives of all types from some of the smallest to some of the largest.

Derby paint shop in 1935 with, nearest the camera, 2P 4-4-0 No.395 receiving a mirror finish coat of black paint after a 'general'. Behind and to the right are brand new Stanier 3P 2-6-2 tanks Nos.91 and 92. The shop is well stocked with various other Derby products and two interesting items of rolling stock; the LMS Dynamometer Car and, just beyond the central columns, Queen Victoria's 12-wheel Special Saloon which is now part of the National Collection. The Royal saloon was built at Wolverton in 1869 as two separate 6-wheel vehicles and later joined together to run on twin 6-wheel bogies. Besides being probably the quietest 'shop' in the works, the Paint Shop would be the cleanest and most secure. Authors collection.

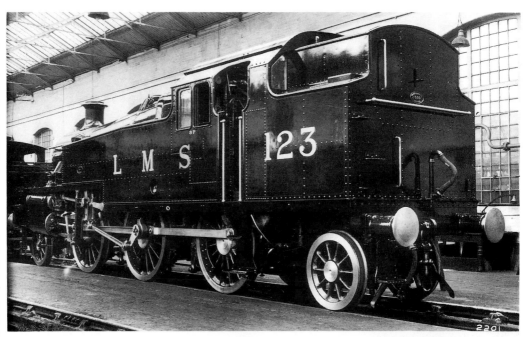

(right) New Stanier 2-6-2T 123 is complete, painted, burnished and ready for work in this September 1935 view inside the paint shop. The craftsmanship of the builders and painters is apparent from this angle but the class, as a whole, was never one of Stanier's better designs. Authors collection.

(middle) Another long-time resident of Derby Paint Shop was the preserved ex-MR 1P 4-2-2 No.118, the last of the eighty five strong class introduced by Johnson in 1887 and built in batches up to 1899. As LMS 673, the single had been withdrawn only four years previous to this 1932 photograph and restored to its original number and Midland livery. Alongside is MR Compound No.1026 finished in crimson lake paint after a 'general'. Locofotos.

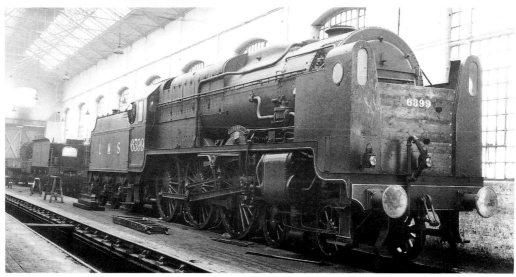

(bottom) Derby had probably the largest paint shop of any railway locomotive works in Britain; there was not as many roads as inside Crewe Paint Shop but the high pitched roof gave a feeling of space as well as the wide working areas between tracks. By the 1930s there was probably some over capacity at the LMS main works and so enclosed areas such as the paint shop at Derby became ideal places to store special items of rolling stock or locomotives as seen in the previous pictures. Whilst the high-pressure 4-6-0 No.6399 FURY, seen fitted with 'indicator shelter', was being tested in 1932 it was kept under cover in the paint shop between its forays out onto the main line. Locofotos.

Between 1924 and 1928 the LMS received, from various workshops and private builders, more than five hundred 4F 0-6-0 goods tender engines, ordered to a former Midland Railway design of 1911, deemed by the then powers-that-be as the best available. Derby's share of this engine building bonanza amounted to more than one hundred and fifty engines and we see 4260 of Order No.6473 being put together in No.2 bay of the erecting shop in 1926. These locomotives were of course 'old-hat' to the Derby men - they had been making them for years. In the war years of 1939 to 1941 they built thirty more of the type to join the 700-odd already at work on the LMS. BR.

New construction during 1929 included three batches of Fowler 2-6-4 tank engines Nos.2325 to 2374. On 29th August we see the last but few members of batch O/7237 being erected. 2371 and 2372, nearest camera, are still only frames but 2369 and 2370 are not too far off completion. When ready they will be lifted onto the centre road and wheeled out of the shop ready for testing and painting. Through the arches on the right can be glimpsed the Machine Shop. Authors collection.

No.2 bay of the Erecting Shop in September 1938 with, nearest camera, two Midland Division based 'Jubilee' 4-6-0s, Nos.5659 DRAKE (Derby built 1934) and 5608 GIBRALTAR. Behind them, on the same road, is a 0-6-0 'Dock' tank, Stanier Class 5, a 4F 0-6-0 and, way up near the doorway, a Stanier 2-6-4T. Two unidentified frames take up the left hand road in front of LMS Compound No.937 and behind that, a number of unidentified locos of various classes. The centre (access) road is taken up by Stanier 2-6-4T 2425, another Derby product of 1936. The 2-6-4T became something of a Derby 'speciality' during Stanier's term as C.M.E. a trend carried on by his successors right into BR days with hundreds of the type constructed there. Note that two new overhead travelling cranes, of 50 tons capacity, now straddle No.2 bay. Crane equipment in the three bays of the Erecting Shop by this time comprised five of 50 tons, three of 35 tons and two of 10 tons. British Railways.

A crane operators view of the Derby erecting shops in 1898 with no less than twenty seven locomotives occupying No.2 bay. Nos. 1 and 3 bays are similarly well patronised. Notice how tidy the working areas were kept. Authors collection.

During the early 1950's 159 ex-LNER Class J39 0-6-0s were 'shopped' at Derby. They came from all parts of the East Coast system and received both 'Intermediate' and 'general' overhauls. Here 64984, from 36A Doncaster shed, stands on Derby shed yard on 19th August 1951 after a 'general'. Authors collection.

After its involvement in the Rotherham accident in 1948, 'Jubilee' 5609 GILBERT AND ELLICE ISLANDS was towed to Derby for eventual repair. Here, on 22nd May of that year, the battered engine and tender await 'shopping'. H.C.Casserley.

27th September 1956 and 58100 is intact and looking none the worse from her July ordeal but it was not to last and even though preservation was muted the engine was dismantled after the Open Day. Peter Groom.

(opposite bottom) *The 0-10-0 Lickey Banker or 'Big Bertha' was arguably Derby's most famous single product and after withdrawal from service in the Spring of 1956, it languished on the 'Scrap Road' at Derby until July of that year when a start was made to dismantle the unique engine. However with the 'Works Open Day' approaching at the end of Summer, a decision was made to include the locomotive as one of the exhibits and 58100 was hastily put back together for the event. In this view taken on 3rd July, the boiler cladding has been stripped as a preliminary move to scrapping. Peter Groom.*

58100's massive cylinder block is lifted from its frame for the last time in early 1957, calls for its preservation went unheeded. Authors collection.

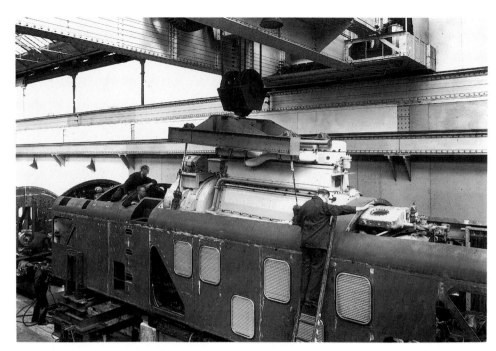

DERBY WORKS

Occupants 2nd November 1952

LOCO	SHED	REPAIR
ERECTING SHOP		
40063	26A	GEN.
40068	5D	GEN
40069	2E	INT
40419	16A	INT
40503	18C	GEN (a)
40692	9D	COL
40937	26C	GEN
41068	20A	GEN
41114	6G	CAS
41164	6A	GEN
41167	5A	GEN
42305	4B	GEN
42326	21A	INT
42328	33A	INT
42373	16A	INT
42380	20E	INT
42402	11B	GEN
42512	33A	GEN
42514	33A	GEN
42527	33A	GEN
43605	18D	GEN
43657	8B	INT
43917	18A	INT
43925	17D	GEN
43950	19C	CAS
43998	18B	INT
44179	21A	INT
44298	14A	GEN
44321	18B	INT
44430	18B	INT
47231	17B	INT
7419	20E	GEN
47562	20F	INT
47626	18D	INT
48272	16D	GEN
48376	15A	INT
48387	15A	INT
48635	16A	GEN
48643	16D	INT
64738	39A	GEN
64764	30A	GEN
64774	30A	INT
64809	39B	INT
64972	37A	INT
73022	6A	CAS
73029	24E	CAS
80005	NEW	Ord 5124
80006	NEW	Ord 5124
80007	NEW	Ord 5124
PAINT/DIESEL SHOP		
43282	8B	exGEN
43753	15C	exGEN
47421	20C	exINT
64745	39A	exGEN
10001	-	STORE
10100	-	STORE
12002	5B	ATT
12032	1A	ATT
12034	5B	GEN
12052	5B	INT
13003	NEW	—
13004	NEW	—
13005	NEW	—
13006	NEW	—
13007	NEW	—
13008	NEW	—
13009	NEW	—
13010	NEW	—
15004	31B	GEN

With the coming of the diesel engine Derby became responsible for building first, the 0-6-0 shunting types (from 1939) and eventually, main line diesel locomotives in the late 1950s. Derby was, it must be remembered, responsible for building the first British main-line diesel locomotives, 10000 and 10001, on the eve of Nationalisation and with the skills accumulated prior to the Modernisation Plan of 1955 it was inevitable that the workshops would get a large share of the orders on offer. In July 1958 Derby completed the first of a batch of 1160 h.p. diesel electric Bo-Bo Type 2 locomotives. D5000 was the loco and in this view taken in mid May 1958 we see the engine and generator being coaxed into the body of the locomotive. Derby turned out this Type 2 design, uprated to 1250 h.p. in 1963, until 1967 when the last one, D7677 entered service. British Railways.

(below) In 1958/59 the first of the Sulzer Type 4 'Peaks', D1 to D10, were completed at Derby. The class of ten became Class 44 in later years and on their introduction worked main-line express passenger trains mainly on the WCML until they were all gathered together at Toton depot where for the rest of their working lives they hauled heavy freight trains. This view in the erecting shop in July 1958 shows one of the massive bogies made for the 138 ton diesel-electric locomotives; alongside and in for repair are 4F 44477 and Stanier 8F 48011. Steam was still being built here up to the middle of the previous year when BR Standard Class 5 No.73154 had the honour of being the last of nearly 3,000 steam locos built by Derby Works. Over a thousand diesels were also constructed here. Some tens of thousands of steam locomotive repairs were carried out over the 112 years that Derby was responsible for that particular form of motive power. G.Whittaker.

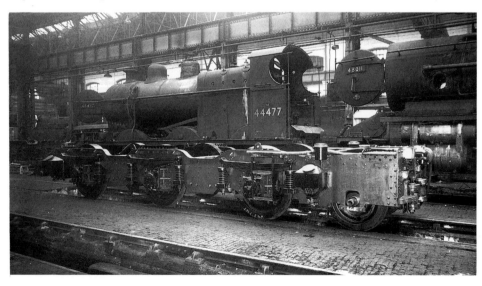

STRIPPING SHED

40523	22B	FOR CUT-UP
41516	17B	INT
47356	1B	GEN
48181	15A	GEN

KLONDYKE SIDINGS

118	-	Preserved
40743	15D	FOR CUT-UP
41000	17A	For Pres.
41044	15D	FOR CUT-UP
41961	16D	FOR CUT-UP
48007	18A	CAS
48197	18A	INT
58231	21A	FOR CUT-UP
64718	39A	GEN
64959	30A	GEN
70373	WD	ex Overseas
508	WD	ex Overseas
512	WD	ex Overseas

DEADMANS LANE Arrival Sidings

40699	12A	COL
41124	6G	INT
43960	20F	INT
44168	17D	INT
44404	20A	Frame weld
47616	5B	GEN
64752	32B	ATT
64800	32B	ATT
64980	38A	GEN

Ex WORKS on DERBY SHED

40034	14B	ex GEN
41093	6G	ex GEN
42524	33C	ex INT
43194	71H	ex GEN
44559	71G	ex GEN
64820	37A	ex INT

Totals:	**Works**	**9 4**
	Shed	**6**

Key:
ATT - Attention to specific fault.
CAS - Casual repair.
COL - Collision damage.
GEN - General repair.
INT - Intermediate repair.
(a) Due General repair but withdrawn.

(above) Open Days at Derby Locomotive Works, organised by the Works Horticultural Society, always attracted large crowds and to entertain both the enthusiast and the curious various displays would be arranged and in his view of the erecting shop during a late 1950's event 4F 44232 is hoisted above the crowd by two of the shop's overhead travelling cranes. L.R.Peters.

(right) The Fell diesel locomotive was built at Derby in 1950 and trials were conducted over the ensuing years to test its potential for hauling express passenger trains. Although it could do what was asked of it on the main line the locomotive suffered mechanical problems at various times and was rarely seen outside Derby Works. 10100 is seen here in April 1954 during one of its long sojourns in the works. In 1958 a major internal fire put paid to any future the unique diesel mechanical locomotive may have had and it was cut-up at Derby in the early months of 1960. L.R.Peters.

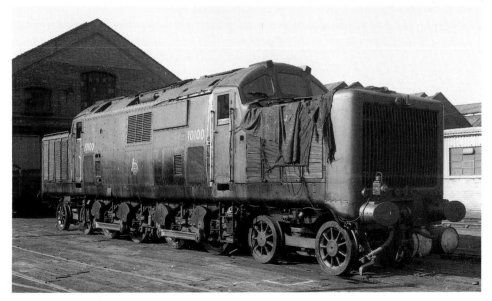

(left) The building of 0-6-0 diesel-electric shunters was an on-going occupation at Derby from 1939 to 1960 when their last example of this once numerous class, D4010, was turned out. After that time all new construction was exclusively main-line locomotives. In this 1956 view, we see the control cabinet being lowered into 13216 (later D3216), in the then No.7, Diesel Erecting Shop which was originally part of the Paint Shop. Authors collection.

(below) An overall view of the diesel bay, looking west, in 1963 with twelve Type 2's in varying stages of construction. These are some of the uprated 1250 h.p. examples which in later years became Class 25's. The No.1 or south bay of the erecting shop was partitioned off from the rest of No.8 shop in order to keep some of the dirt from the steam locomotive repairs contaminating the more sensitive workings of the diesel locomotives. It is difficult to realise that none of these locomotives, which were at the forefront of railway technology only thirty years ago, are now all gone except for a few examples in preservation. Authors collection.

DONCASTER

'The Plant', as Doncaster Locomotive Works was known locally, was responsible for producing some of the most famous steam locomotives ever to grace our railway system. Probably the greatest period of production was during the Gresley era when the 3-cylinder Pacific's of the A1, A3 and A4 classes were built to haul the express passenger trains of the LNER at a time when competition between railway companies was as fierce in the 1930's as it is today between the airlines. Established in 1853, when the Great Northern Railway moved its main locomotive repair facility from Boston, Doncaster Works continued to expand over the years and by 1867 was building its first locomotives. By the turn of the century the works had basically reached their ultimate size and covered some 61 acres of which 13 were under cover. The Crimpsall shops became the main locomotive repair building and though somewhat detached from the main manufacturing shops centred around the old works complex, there was plenty of room for expansion. The sprawling yards also made photography easier when compared with some other locomotive works.

Steam locomotive production spanned a ninety year period to 1957 when BR Standard Class 4 no.76114 steamed out of 'The Plant' as the last in a long line of distinguished and mostly successful locomotives.

Steam railcar BANG UP visits the boiler repair bay of Crimpsall erecting shop in September 1934. A.W.Croughton.

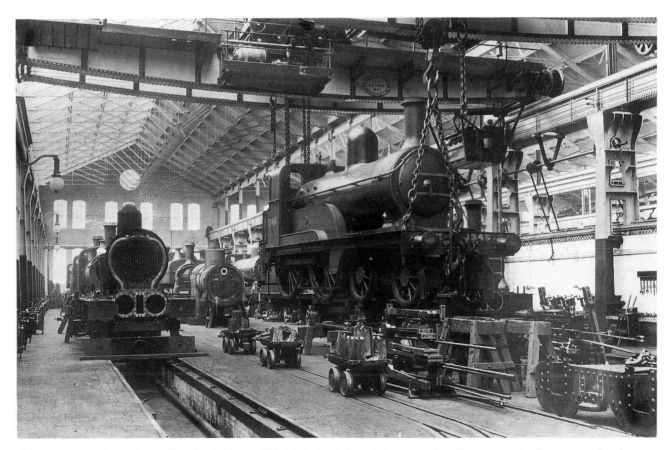

Crimpsall repair shops about 1908 with GN Class D2 4-4-0 No.1345 slung between the two 35 tons capacity Cravens overhead cranes supplied for the opening of these shops in 1901. The Ivatt D2, built in 1898, was one of those rebuilt by Gresley to GN Class D3 and enjoyed a working life of 50 years being withdrawn in January 1949 carrying its 1946 LNER number, 2137. Authors collection.

No.4 Bay of Crimpsall repair shops at the end of the LNER era with an unidentified A3 being stripped on the centre road whilst to its left is a Thompson B1 having work done to its front-end. It is a Thursday morning, the date 19th June 1947 and the LNER are busy catching up on repairs deferred during the conflict of WW2. The amount of dirt on the floor and in the pits is reminiscent of the average back street garage. This view is looking north-east, the main yard being through the sunlit doorway. Alec Swain.

Gresley A4 QUICKSILVER entered "The Plant" for a 'casual light' repair on the 8th January 1959 and here, some three days later, inside Crimpsall shops awaits attention. Leaving at the end of the month and returning to Kings Cross, its home shed, 60015 came back to Doncaster Works less than six weeks later for a 'general'. In May 1963 it returned to "The Plant" for the last time - for cutting-up. N.E.Stead.

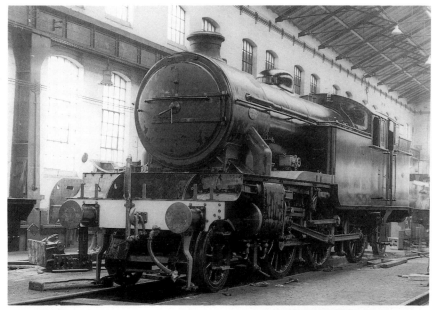

V1 No.461 nears completion in the 'New Erecting Shop' in April 1936. This shop was some distance away from the main (Crimpsall) shops and was situated near to the manufacturing shops in the works. Completed at the end of the Great Northern era, under Gresley's charge, this shop went on to build hundreds of locomotives over the ensuing years and up to the 1980's was still building large diesel locomotives for British Rail. Back in 1936, 461 was one of eighteen 2-6-2 tank locomotives built to Order No.337. W.L.Good.

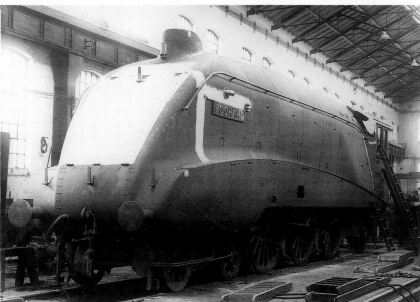

Probably Doncaster's most famous locomotive class was the Gresley A4's. Between 1935 and 1938 thirty-five of the streamlined Pacific's were built here and on 27th March 1938 No.4499 POCHARD was all but complete. Entering traffic some sixteen days later and allocated to Gateshead shed, 4499 was not to keep its wildfowl name because just a year after completion it was renamed after the LNER Deputy Chairman of Directors - SIR MURROUGH WILSON. Condemned in May 1964 as 60002 the engine had eleven different boilers during its twenty-six year life but kept the same tender, non-corridor 5673, throughout. W.L.Good.

One of the diminutive locomotive types emerging from Doncaster in BR days was the 204 horsepower 0-6-0 diesel mechanical shunters. Between 1957 and 1962, more than two hundred of these useful locomotives were constructed at Doncaster and Swindon Works. D2388, a Doncaster example photographed on Sunday 26th March 1961, stands in the yard outside the New Erecting Shop ready for its short journey to the Paint Shop the following morning. Wearing nothing more than primer and filler here, D2388 was sent to Birkenhead two weeks later in full Brunswick green livery and striped ends. After just over ten years service and with the work it was designed to do diminishing, it was withdrawn and sold for scrap. Authors collection.

An overall view of the 'New Erecting Shop' on Monday 8th April 1957 with BR Standard Class 5 4-6-0's and tenders for the Standard Class 4 2-6-0's of the 76XXX number series being built. The place is a hive of activity and the locomotives are seen in various stages of building. Nearest the camera and nearly complete is probably 73169 completed 26th April, whilst others of the same class flank it. Doncaster was responsible for building 122 BR Standards, 42 Class 5's, 70 Class 4's and 10 of the Class 4 2-6-4T of the 8XXXX series. The Class 4's Nos.76100 to 76114 were to be the last steam locomotives built at Doncaster and in the following October No.76114, completed, rolled out with due ceremony to follow the 2,222 engines that had gone before it. British Railways.

In 1960 Doncaster received an order to build forty Class AL5 Bo-Bo electric locomotives for the London Midland Region's West Coast Main Line electrification. Numbered E3056 - E3095, they later became Class 85. The first electric emerged from Doncaster in June 1961 and the last AL5 was delivered in late 1964 but before that left the 'New Erecting Shop', Doncaster had received another order for AC electric locomotives, this time for forty of the AL6 Class (Class 86) which were delivered in 1965/66. This view shows one of the early members of the AL5's being put together in late 1960. British Railways.

With its nameplates and numbers still to be applied ANDREW K.McKOSH undergoes a repaint on Thursday 19th June 1947 after a 'general' repair. Garter Blue, its pre-war livery, with red and white lining is being applied after the nearly five years of war-time unlined black paint. Within three days the locomotive will be handed back to the Operating Department and returned to traffic. The 'northlight' roof of the Paint Shop was so constructed to give maximum natural light with minimum glare. Alec Swain.

(below) It was usual for locomotives that had completed repairs at Doncaster to be hauled down to the shed for steaming and a cavalcade of usually four or five engines left 'The Plant' a couple of times each week for the short journey to the running shed. Three such engines, still coupled together, were on the shed yard on Sunday 4th June 1950; the pristine black paintwork of the two N2's and V2 no.60872, in marked contrast to other engines on the yard. On the extreme left A4 no.60006 which had left the Works on the previous Wednesday after a 'general', sports the blue livery with black and white lining. L.R.Peters.

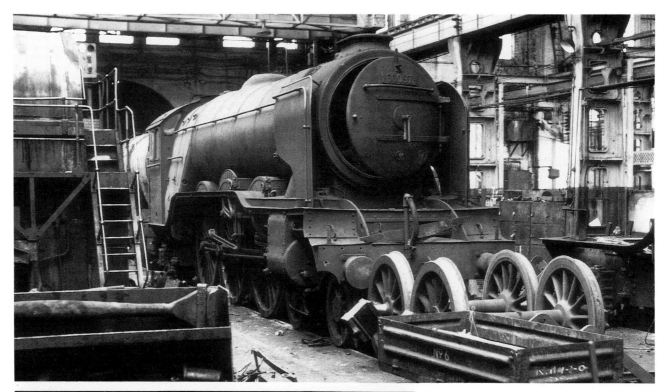

(above) 60097 HUMORIST was the only A3 to be fitted with this type of smoke deflectors. On 29th December 1961 the engine came to Doncaster for its last 'general' repair, departing on 9th February 1962 to St Margarets shed where it had just been re-allocated from Haymarket prior to its visit to Doncaster. This Sunday 14th January 1962 view, inside No.2 bay of Crimpsall shops, shows that it had suffered some collision damage to the front right bufferbeam probably the reason for its two week sojourn in the works yard before repairs were commenced. Unusually for a Scottish Region based engine, 60097 was cut-up at Doncaster, in late summer 1963; after entering for a 'general' in July of that year HUMORIST was condemned on the 24th August. N.E.Stead.

(centre opposite) Having performed its test run without any problems, 60079 BAYARDO spends a Saturday on Doncaster shed yard before working north to its home shed at Carlisle Canal. The A3 had just completed a 'general' repair on the previous Thursday 12th June 1958 having entered 'shops' on the 8th May. This 'general' was to be the locomotive's penultimate, it had another in late 1959 and on a return to Doncaster in September 1961 it was condemned and cut-up. This picture reminds us how splendid these engines looked after a visit to the paint shop. A.G.Ellis

(left) After painting, locomotives went to the Weigh House before leaving the 'Plant'. Having just completed a 'general', N2 69530 of Hornsey has some adjustments made on the 8th April 1957 before its journey south. Authors collection.

Sunday 25th June 1939 and brand new V2 No.4845 adorns the yard alongside the weigh house. This was Doncaster's 1,900th locomotive and was released to traffic on the following Tuesday, its first shed being Doncaster. W.L.Good.

(right) BR Standard Class 5 no.73162 on the works yard in May 1959 after a repair and repaint. The Huddersfield based engine had been turned out from Doncaster only two years previously and was amongst the last steam locomotives built there. L.R.Peters.

Pioneer Ivatt 'Large Atlantic' or C1 class No.251 outside the weigh house in Great Northern days and probably shortly after completion as it wears the original trailing wheel springs and the non-standard chimney first applied. W.B.Yeadon collection.

To move locomotive boilers between the main boiler shop and the erecting shops, old locomotive and tender chassis were employed. On a murky 30th April 1961 one of the two C1 Atlantic frames still used by Doncaster for this job was captured on film in the yard. The C1 frames were probably the only surviving Atlantic frames at that time. P.B.Booth per N.E.Stead collection.

In June 1950 steam for the works was being supplied by 'Stationary Boilers' 845 and 844, still attached to withdrawn C1 Atlantic's 3274 and 3285. To hold the maximum amount of coal, both tenders had built up side sheets and interestingly, considering the amount of fixed pipework and large chimney extensions, both locomotives appear capable of moving under their own power as the connecting rods are still in place. The C1's carried out this duty for many years and were not finally retired until March 1952. L.R.Peters.

The River Don ran alongside the north-west boundary of Doncaster Works and a stroll along the river bank in the 1950's would have brought this sight into view. The five ex-locomotive boilers comprised the Smiths Shop and West Carriage Shop heating plant and on this date, 17th May 1953, were made up from Class C1 Atlantic's. The Stationary Boiler numbers listed below are followed by the locomotive number in brackets followed by the date in use for works heating duties: SB 790 (ex4444) 8/46 to 12/65; SB 798 (ex3296) 8/46 to 12/65; SB 796 (ex4437) 8/46 to 7/65; SB 809 (ex4434) 6/47 to 12/65; SB 810 (ex4413) 10/47 to 8/61. N.E.Stead.

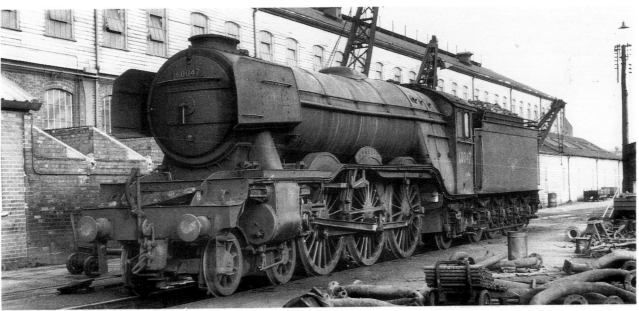

Visitors on the 14th January 1962 saw New England based 60047 DONOVAN was in Doncaster Works for a 'casual light' repair and is standing on the south side of Crimpsall shops where the following morning it would have been parted from its tender and moved forward to the traverser ready for entry into the shops. Although filthy dirty the engine still looks handsome with its recently fitted German-type smoke deflectors. N.E.Stead.

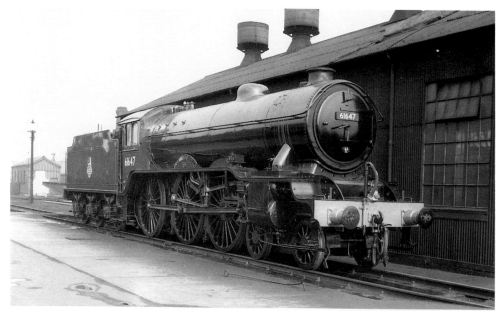

In the same week that B17 61624 was being cut-up (see page 48), sister engine 61647 had just completed a 'general' repair. Seen alongside the Weigh House on the 12th April, the B17 would be released to traffic and return to its shed at Ipswich on the following day. L.R.Peters.

K1 62038 appears to be in dire straights in this June 1950 photograph but it was only being got ready to enter the Erecting Shop for repair. L.R.Peters.

Although Doncaster did not build any main-line diesel locomotives until well after steam had disappeared from our railway system, it did receive, for acceptance trails, many of the new diesel types that were being introduced in the late 1950's and early 60's. Here Brush Type 2 D5531, two Type 1's D6112 and D6110 and an unidentified Baby Deltic stand on the Paint Shop yard on the 23rd May 1959 after delivery from their various manufacturers. L.R.Peters.

One activity performed at Doncaster virtually without pause during the days of steam was the cutting up of locomotives. This view across the river towards the Crimpsall in May 1959 shows a variety of engines awaiting the cutter's torch. Up to 1958 it was mainly ex-LNER locomotives seen on these scrap roads but as withdrawals grew on BR (sometimes hundreds every month) so the types of locomotives grew more diverse. Many of the ex-LMS engines formerly working on the London, Tilbury & Southend line found their way to Doncaster, ex-MR 2P 4-4-0's, ex-Somerset & Dorset 2-8-0's and other LMS types. The number of withdrawn engines had grown to tremendous proportions by 1960 and private scrapyards began to purchase everything they could get their hands on. However Doncaster's appetite for scrap did not diminish until 1964 and up to that time they certainly scrapped a lot of famous and not-so-famous locomotives. This was the period when you could purchase A3 nameplates from BR for £18 or £20 each depending on their weight! N.E.Stead.

The scrapyard in May 1936 with ex-GER 4-4-0 no.8027 and 2-4-0 no.7473 heading a line of condemned engines. The E4 had been withdrawn during the previous December from Ipswich shed whilst the D13, formely of Norwich shed, had been condemned in January. Authors collection.

On 23rd May 1937 ex-Great Central locomotives, amongst others, awaiting scrap on the Crimpsall. D7 No.5692 with sister 5683 behind, are stripped of anything useful. W.L.Good

B17 no.61624 was condemned at Doncaster Works on 16th March 1953 and was being cut-up by 12th April. The photograph offers an interesting view of the inside cylinder block. L.R.Peters.

One of the works shunters on the 12th April 1953 was J52 no.68845 in the guise of Departmental No.1. Doncaster had a leaning towards ex Great Northern engines performing this duty right up to the end of steam repairs. L.R.Peters.

EASTLEIGH

This works will always be best remembered, in the later steam period at least, as the place responsible for the repair and maintenance of the Southern 'Pacific' classes. Just as Doncaster took care of the LNER pacific's and Crewe the LMS 4-6-2's then Eastleigh took sole charge for the regular 'shopping' of the Merchant Navy and West Country/Battle of Britain engines working on the Southern *(see pages 52 and 53 for 1958 'shopping list)*. But Eastleigh had more to offer than the 4-6-2's; other famous names such as the King Arthur and Lord Nelson classes graced the erecting shop floor as well as the more mundane and everyday workhorses from all over the south of England.

Established by the London & South Western Railway in 1910 on a 'green field site', Eastleigh became the most important of the three locomotive workshops (the others being Ashford and Brighton) on the Southern Railway after Grouping. In total more than 400 locomotives were built there over a forty year period (about half up to 1923) and many thousands repaired. Both LMS and BR standard types became regular visitors for heavy repairs in the late 1950's and early 60's. With the closure of Ashford and Brighton, Eastleigh took on sole responsibility for the maintenance of all Southern Region based locomotives including the diesel and electric locomotives that were to oust steam in the late 1960's.

In a typical month something like forty locomotives would enter the works for 'shopping' with up to a dozen 4-6-2's amongst them. Curiously Eastleigh was never entrusted with construction of any of the BR Standard classes, Brighton taking on this role of the SR share.

Although surviving today in a much reduced status, the works continues to service the electric multiple unit fleet of the SR.

T9 no.119 inside the paint shop on 30th June 1935 wearing a special paint finish and plaques of the royal coat-of-arms on the leading splashers. The engine had been designated for working royal and special trains and on this date was being got ready to haul the train conveying King George V to the Silver Jubilee Naval Review at Spithead on the 2nd July. Even after WW2 and as 30119 this locomotive was committed to special duties. During its lifetime the T9 had steamed over one and half million miles and was finally scrapped at Ashford in 1952. H.C.Casserley.

Twenty seven years later on 30th August 1952 in the No.2 bay of the erecting shop another T9 looks nearly as resplendent in the BR livery of the period as it completes a 'general'. Behind are two Pacifics stripped of their casing in readiness for repair. L.R.Peters.

The Q1's were never candidates for the best looking steam locomotives and in this September 1947 view of C22, the absence of the middle set of driving wheels does nothing to enhance its ugly appearance. To the right of the engine is the boiler repair bay, the western end of the same bay was dedicated to tender repair. H.C.Casserley.

Visitors admire 'West Country' 34101 HARTLAND as it begins to take shape during the final phase of its rebuilding in August 1960. The rebuilding of the Southern Region Pacifics was carried out over a number of years and each locomotive could be resident in the erecting shop from 4 to 8 weeks depending on work load and part availability. L.R.Peters.

Eastleigh Erecting Shop 22/10/61. It seems that ladders, like hand tools, will walk if left alone for long enough and so it was the practice of the Eastleigh fitters to paint their names on such items that they had been issued with to at least prevent such amazing feats of 'magic'. At least L.Shepherd would have been able to carry on stripping Q class 30538 when he returned to the erecting shop on Monday 23rd October 1961. P.B.Booth.

On the same weekend other residents of the shop included M7 30480 and K 32343. The lifting strops used for lifting and moving these locomotives about the shop are arranged on the right. Like most pieces of equipment in the 'shops' the strops would belong to that particular bay, never moving across the boundary into the next bay for fear of being 'lost'. P.B.Booth.

Most of the BR Standard Class 5's working on the SR were named after Arthurian characters and 73119 ELAINE, in the company of 30863 LORD RODNEY, undergoes an 'intermediate' repair in August 1960. L.R.Peters collection.

Eastleigh Works 1958

Southern Region Pacific locomotive repairs. Listed in order of arrival.
First tender number is that attached to loco on arrival, second number is that
with which loco departed.
Repair key: G - General; H/C - Heavy Casual; H/I - Heavy Intermediate; L/C -
Light Casual; L/I - Light Intermediate; M - Modification; N/C - Non Classified;
Works Holiday 14th to 28th July.
Mileage is that recorded since last 'general'.
The WC/BB and MN Pacific's accounted for approximately 25% of the
Eastleigh locomotive repair throughput in each year.

Loco	Tender	Date In	Date Out	Repair	Mileage
34106	????/3272	29/11/57	3/1/58	L/I	82,082
34012	3272/3368	4/12/57	17/1	G+M	189,519
35022	——	5/12/57	11/1	L/I	123,134
34049	——	6/12/57	11/1	L/I	7,805
34018	——	11/12/57	10/1	L/C	190,517
34092	3352/3305	16/12/57	11/1	H/I	64,126
34004	3305/3352	19/12/57	1/2	G+M	220,963
34036	——	20/12/57	18/1	L/I	134,446
34095	——	1/1/58	25/1	L/I	133,953
34104	3364/3304	3/1	25/1	H/I	70,121
34035	——	7/1	1/2	L/I	158,996
35003	——	8/1	1/2	L/I	157,010
34026	3304/3364	9/1	15/2	G+M	203,949
34037	3268/3330	14/1	1/3	G+M	193,761
34059	——	16/1	8/2	H/I	140,387
34051	——	17/1	15/2	L/I	144,989
34024	——	24/1	21/2	L/I	151,670
34079	3330/3268	29/1	22/2	L/I	179,516
70014	——	30/1	14/2	N/C	64,691
34084	——	3/2	1/3	H/I	129,030
34074	3324/3257	5/2	7/3	L/I	165,919
34107	——	7/2	14/2	N/C	100,351
34014	3257/3324	10/2	15/3	G+M	154,114
35020	——	11/2	8/3	L/I	113,007
34066	——	17/2	22/3	H/C	133,321
35022	——	17/2	22/2	L/C	124,184
34055	——	20/2	14/3	L/I	68,839
35004	——	21/2	26/2	N/C	142,890
34088	3339/3255	24/2	22/3	L/I	107,020
34016	3255/3339	25/2	5/4	G+M	223,960
34078	——	25/2	29/3	H/I	178,886
35013	——	6/3	29/3	L/I	116,883
34085	——	7/3	5/4	L/I	167,910
35030	——	12/3	23/4	G+M	143,459
35005	——	13/3	2/4	L/C	183,644
34071	——	14/3	12/4	L/I	137,131
34082	——	17/3	18/4	L/I	180,561
34097	——	21/3	19/4	L/I	115,496
35021	——	25/3	25/4	H/I	203,188
35002	——	28/3	10/5	G+M	161,982
34067	——	31/3	10/5	G	161,956
34102	——	8/4	3/5	L/I	70,598
34099	——	11/4	9/5	L/I	114,457
35007	——	15/4	31/5	G+M	183,787
34070	——	17/4	24/5	G	136,455
34100	——	18/4	2/5	L/C	105,542
35023	——	22/4	10/5	L/C	92,374
34058	——	23/4	23/5	H/I	147,661
34030	——	29/4	24/5	H/I	90,704
34037	——	29/4	24/5	L/C	4,700
35015	3343/3123	1/5	14/6	G+M	133,392
35024	3123/3343	5/5	14/5	L/C	223,158
34101	——	7/5	7/6	L/I	85,192
35010	——	8/5	31/5	L/I	95,448
35018	——	14/5	14/6	L/I	141,359
35004	——	16/5	5/7	G+M	156,914
34006	——	20/5	21/6	H/I	151,879
35017	——	20/5	21/6	H/I	80,758
34069	——	22/5	27/6	H/I	220,480
35002	——	30/5	20/6	N/C	868
35014	——	2/6	28/6	L/I	137,765
34028	3279/3370	4/6	9/8	G+M	224,585
34110	3370/3279	10/6	2/8	G	147,966
34063	——	17/6	16/8	G	233,888
35005	——	18/6	29/7	H/C	196,167
34050	3256/3353	20/6	29/8	G+M	190,588
34019	——	24/6	2/8	L/I	106,814
34038	——	26/6	9/8	L/I	155,487
35006	——	1/7	16/8	L/I	253,172
34098	3353/3256	4/7	23/8	L/I	158,935
34052	3293/3323	10/7	13/9	G+M	194,754
Works Holiday period 20-7 to 3/8 incl.					
34045	3298/3327	29/7	17/10	G+M	54,863
34057	——	31/7	30/8	H/I	87,518
35028	——	6/8	6/9	L/I	143,009
34018	3259/3340	7/8	27/9	G+M	216,997
34086	3340/3298	11/8	27/8	L/C	154,832
34077	3327/3259	12/8	6/9	L/I	185,269
35009	——	15/8	13/9	L/I	114,363
34008	——	20/8	20/9	L/I	156,172
35029	——	25/8	13/9	L/C	181,115
34073	3323/3293	26/8	4/10	G	173,381
34044	——	29/8	20/9	L/I	202,305
34105	3361/3252	4/9	4/10	L/I	126,620
34047	3252/3361	10/9	1/11	G+M	233,152
34094	——	15/9	11/10	L/I	143,871
34103	3363/3307	19/9	18/10	H/I	121,821
35016	——	25/9	18/10	L/I	101,610
34053	3307/3363	26/9	15/11	G+M	151,810
34015	——	29/9	25/10	L/I	85,018
34039	——	7/10	10/10	N/C	260,274
35011	——	9/10	25/10	L/C	154,086
34031	3282/3354	10/10	29/11	G+M	213,605
34100	3354/3282	14/10	8/11	L/I	124,684
34033	——	16/10	8/11	H/I	94,563
35026	——	20/10	8/11	L/I	128,908
35019	——	24/10	8/11	L/C	158,087
34029	3251/3356	27/10	13/12	G+M	198,435
34046	——	27/10	1/11	L/C	195,505
34093	3356/3251	30/10	22/11	L/I	164,108
34068	——	31/10	13/12	G	183,870
34011	——	6/11	6/12	H/I	77,429
35003	——	7/11	29/11	L/C	210,582
34042	3301/3334	11/11	2/1/59	G+M	194,476
34005	——	14/11	29/11	H/C	56,022
34040	——	18/11	13/12	L/I	128,957
34023	——	19/11	20/12	L/I	140,062
35029	——	21/11	13/12	L/C	190,401
35008	——	25/11	20/12	L/I	119,725
34039	——	26/11	17/1/59	G+M	261,020
34083	3334/3301	27/11	10/1/59	G	199,694
35012	——	2/12	24/12	L/I	116,773
34061	——	4/12	9/1/59	L/I	167,119
35011	——	5/12	13/12	L/C	159,051
34056	——	10/12	17/1/59	L/I	160,226
34010	——	12/12	31/1/59	G+M	171,903
35025	——	17/12	10/1/59	L/I	127,340
34082	——	18/12	3/1/59	L/C	197,582
34055	——	23/12	8/1/59	L/C	104,297

During 1958 the following locomotives were cut-up at Eastleigh. Dates shown
are the week-ending.

W/E	Loco	Class
4/1	30757	757
18/1	30708	T9
18/1	30721	T9
1/2	30283	T9
1/2	30588	C14
15/2	30224	O2
22/2	30233	O2
1/3	30162	G6
8/3	30038	M7
15/3	30738	N15
22/3	30675	M7
19/4	30568	0395
26/4	30564	0395
10/5	30284	T9
17/5	30022	M7
24/5	32424	H2
7/6	30037	M7

28/6	30285	T9
2/8	30334	H15
9/8	30242	M7
27/9	30243	M7
4/10	32113	E1
18/10	30727	T9
8/11	30333	H15
22/11	30454	N15
29/11	30260	G6
6/12	30322	M7
20/12	30712	T9

(below) By the time a reconditioned boiler was put onto the frames and a set of retyred wheels, from goodness knows which members of the class, were fitted, there was not much left of the original locomotive. This was Class 700 0-6-0 No.689, already 40 years old, on 15th August 1937 in the throes of a 'general' overhaul. H.C.Casserley.

(bottom) 'BB' 34055 FIGHTER PILOT was one of the 'unrebuilt' members of the class which remained so until withdrawal. Here in October 1961 the Pacific is being got ready for traffic after a 'general'. N.E.Stead collection.

'Schools' class No.937 EPSOM nears completion on 30th June 1935. The following month would see the last two members of this class completed. Behind 937 is Atlantic 2039 HARTLAND POINT a former LBSCR engine of 1906 vintage which survived until 1951 and in on this date is in for a 'general'. H.C.Casserley.

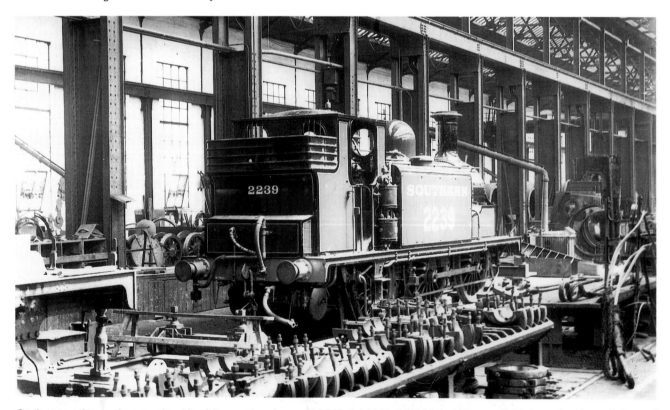

On the same day, on the opposite side of the erecting shop, ex-LBSCR 0-4-2T No.2239 basks in the sunlight streaming through the roof lights. This engine was one of those fitted with fire-fighting equipment during the Second World War and was nearly seventy years old when withdrawn in 1948. H.C.Casserley.

Eastleigh paint shop in September 1932 with Class O4 No.638 and T1 No.16 sharing the tracks with a number of finished and unfinished tenders for the 'Schools' class locomotives then being built. During the Second World War this shop was re-equipped to produce various armaments, locomotives were then painted in the erecting shop and after the ending of hostilities the original paint shop saw another use when it was converted for the repair of electrical components. H.C.Casserley.

Decripit WD 1261, a Porter built USA 0-6-0 tank, was obtained by the Southern Railway in September 1947 but never refurbished for ongoing service like many of its counterparts that found work in Southampton Docks. Two years later, in September 1949, it still languished in Eastleigh yard with a couple of former LNWR tenders, converted to water carriers, as company. 1261's boiler was eventually removed in November of the following year and transferred to sister 30063 whilst the rest of the engine was used for spares or cut-up. L.R.Peters.

An intersting group in the works yard in August 1954 with an unidentified T9, 0-6-0T BOXHILL, now preserved, and 0-4-0ST 30458 IRONSIDE. H.C.Casserley.

GORTON

Gorton Works was bounded on all sides by heavy engineering and by the time of Grouping expansion was impossible and so for the next forty years the place carried on building and repairing locomotives with little or no investment.

During the LNER period new locomotive construction was something of a secondary role for the one and a half thousand workforce employed in its shops. Darlington and Doncaster were designated as the main building works and got the majority of the jobs whilst Gorton was charged with the repair of former Great Central engines and some of the expanding fleet of LNER standard classes. On the south side of the Manchester - Sheffield main line, opposite 'The Tank' as Gorton Works was known locally, stood 'Gorton Foundry', the premises of Beyer Peacock & Co. where locomotive building had been going on for virtually the same amount of time as it had at 'The Tank'. The latter works was virtually the same size as 'The Tank' but being engaged purely in locomotive building, with occasional repair contracts in depressed periods, all its energies and facilities could be focused on construction thus speeding up the process and at a competitive price. The MS&LR and GC both had large numbers of engines built there and so did the LNER, much to the chagrin of the railway workshop personnel across the tracks.

For the enthusiast Gorton Works had much to offer, not necessarily in numbers of engines but in variety. Many of the smaller classes that were scattered about the far reaches of the former LNER system would come for repair. During BR days scrapping became an important source of work and at times the scrapyard played temporary host to allsorts of engines not normally associated with Gorton. Weekly visits were sometimes too infrequent if one was to catch a last glimpse of many that 'passed through' the scrapyard. In the July/August of 1959, former LMS Compound 41101 visited the works for a one-off paint job - yellow and black - so that the locomotive could haul a Bank Holiday "Andy Capp" special, sponsored by a national newspaper, from Manchester to Blackpool. Rumour has it that Derby Works could not bring themselves to apply the garish livery in the first place and Gorton was entrusted with the task. After the event the engine was immediately taken back to Derby and scrapped.

The run-down of British Railways workshops was no more apparent than at Gorton and closure was inevitable. The Works repaired its last locomotives in 1963, Stanier 8F 48520 had the distinction of being the last steam locomotive whilst EM2 Co-Co 27001 ARIADNE became the last, being returned to traffic on 24th May. Once the adjacent engine shed had been closed the whole site was cleared to make way for Manchester's relocated Smithfield wholesale fruit and vegetable market. Across the tracks 'Gorton Foundry' did not fair any better, with lack of orders Beyer Peacock "Locomotive Builders to the World" closed down and another slice of railway history became just that.

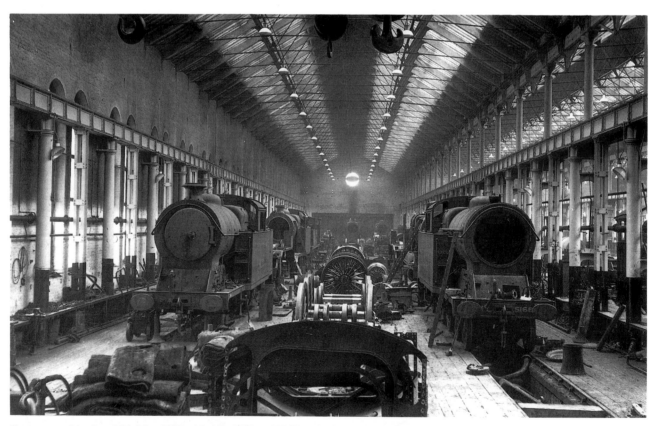

Gorton erecting shop 29th May 1938 with A5's 5030 and 5168 to the fore; other locomotives in for repair include another A5, an O4, B17 no.2838, a couple of tank engines and two ex GC 4-6-0's. Locomotive building had been erratic during the LNER period with only seventy-six locomotives built between 1923 and 1939. BR favoured Gorton with ten B1 4-6-0's, the last steam locomotives to be built there, in 1948/9. The following year and up to 1954 the works was entrusted with the erection of the fifty-seven EM1 Bo-Bo electric locomotives for the Manchester-Sheffield electrification scheme; also the seven larger EM2 Co-Co electric's for the same line. Erection of the electrics was carried out in this bay of the erecting shop during the 1950's and whenever they came in for repair it was always to this same area. W.L.Good.

The erecting shop at Gorton consisted of four 'bays', each bay having three pit roads; two 50 or 40 ton capacity overhead cranes ran the length of each bay. In this July 1948 view N5 no.9315, of Neasden shed, has just arrived and is about to undergo a 'general'. It was another N5, 9274, which had an unfortunate incident here during 1947 when it was being slewed about the shop by two cranes and one of them broke down; unfortunately 9274 was approximately 8 feet off the floor at this time and could not be lowered. Packing, in the form of sleepers, was built up beneath the engine and for the next five weeks the N5 stayed perched on its temporary plinth until the crane was repaired. 9274 was not the only locomotive affected by the breakdown, all the other engines in the bay which were off their wheels were stranded too. L.R.Peters.

(centre) O4 E3713 gets ready to tow J39 E4752 to the paint shop after the latter had just completed a 'general' on Thursday 11th March 1948. The O4 had also just completed a repair and as part of its 'running-in' programme its was performing, amongst other jobs, pilot duties in the works yard. H.C.Casserley.

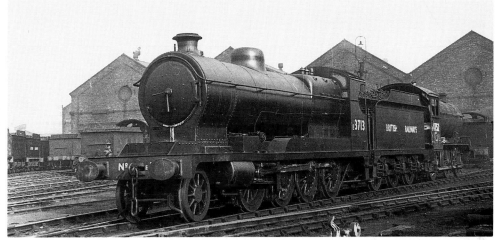

Q4 E3243 is ready for repainting after leaving the erecting shop in March 1948. Its tender has already undergone the necessary work and requires only coal and water. H.C.Casserley.

By 1962 Gorton was repairing mainly WD 2-8-0's, BR 9F 2-10-0's and what remained of LNER classes J39, O1 and O4. These two views of the erecting shop in July 1962 show representatives of three of those classes undergoing repair. At this time nearly 1,500 men were employed in the shops but the run down in locomotive repair had begun and less than a year later Gorton Works was closed and demolished. both N.E.Stead collection.

(right) The Garratt undergoing conversion to oil burning in the summer of 1952. William Lees.

(centre) This view of the Paint Shop on the 30th September 1950 reveals new electric locomotives 26001 and 26002 beside B1 no.61150 which had just completed a 'general' overhaul; B17 61627, at the rear, had also just completed a 'general'. The Paint Shop at Gorton was situated alongside and next door to Gorton engine shed which could not have done much good to new paintwork although with the heavy, polluted atmosphere found in the district it would not have mattered much where the paint shop had been sited. C.A.Appleton.

(below) EM1 26055 beside the Erecting Shop, 19th March 1961, newly painted in lined Brunswick green and named PROMETHEUS. EM1's 26046 to 26057 and all the EM2's were fitted with steam heating boilers and were given names from Greek mythology which was most appropriate as the same names had been used on some of the first locomotives built at Gorton, over a century before, for the Manchester, Sheffield & Lincolnshire Railway. Ian G.Holt.

Sandwiched between J10 5179 and an unidentified J39, Class J60 No.8366 was about to be condemned on this Friday 12th March 1948. The J10 was more fortunate and emerged from shops during the following month complete with BR number 65179. H.C.Casserley.

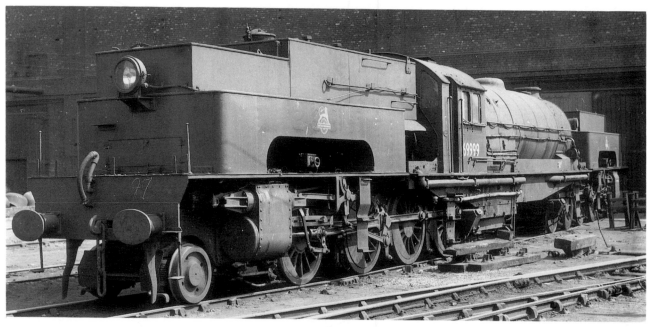

U1 no.69999 the sole LNER Garratt outside the erecting shop in April 1955. Coming towards the end of its chequered BR career, 69999 was at Gorton for a 'non-classified' repair. Virtually residing at the works from 1st February until 28th June, the Garratt was undergoing its last repair before withdrawal. During its LNER career the locomotive had always been 'shopped' at Doncaster, that place being not too far away from its home shed at Mexborough. However with the impending electrification of its usual haunt, the Worsborough branch, its banking capabilities were no longer required and it was sent to the Lickey incline in 1949 where it did a couple of spells first as a coal burning engine and latterly as an oil burner. Because it was a large, unwieldy, one-off, the Garratt could not find favour with its new masters and after spending long periods out of use it was finally withdrawn just two days before Christmas 1955. This yard view gives a good impression of its immense bulk. B.K.B.Green.

The B17's were nothing if not nomadic when 'shopping' was due. In the first instance the LNER concentrated them for repairs at Stratford, then Gorton, then Darlington, back to Stratford, then Gorton and finally Doncaster. Here one of the last members of the class to be built, *2868 BRADFORD CITY*, languishes on the works yard, in late May 1938, after completing a 'general' but still missing various parts before being ready for traffic. Those rebuilt to B2 were repaired by Stratford which works also scrapped them. W.L.Good.

(centre) Q1 no.69926, a former Gorton built Q4 rebuilt in 1942, awaits works in April 1955. The Frodingham based engine would be good for another three years work after its 'non-classified' repair. B.K.B.Green.

Gorton had a its own mark for locomotives that were to be cut-up - the big white X. J10 no.65163 and its tender bore the marks on Sunday the 1st February 1953; by Monday afternoon it would be in pieces on the ground. All the J10's were broken up at Gorton as were most of their larger cousins, the J11's. B.K.B.Green.

(above) By 1962 the workload of repairs at Gorton was diminishing and scrapping was taking precedence. Amongst this group of locomotives waiting to be cut up on 8th July of that year are ex LNER locomotives 63895 and three other O4's sharing the road with a J11 and ex Midland 3F 43763 sandwiched between them. Locofotos.

Two years earlier, on 19th August 1960, former London Midland 0-8-0's nos.48932, 49210 and 49509 had arrived for cutting up. Locofotos.

Expansion of the locomotive works at Gorton was impossible by the turn of the century due to the sprawl of heavy engineering works in the area so at certain times the workload brought overcrowding to the yards and shops. Such was the case in 1948 and 1949 when dozens of withdrawn locomotives were stored at Dukinfield carriage works until they could be dealt with at Gorton. In mid June 1949 B9 no.61475 and F2 no.7104, both withdrawn in the previous month, await the inevitable outside the wartime camouflaged carriage shops at Dukinfield. H.C.Casserley.

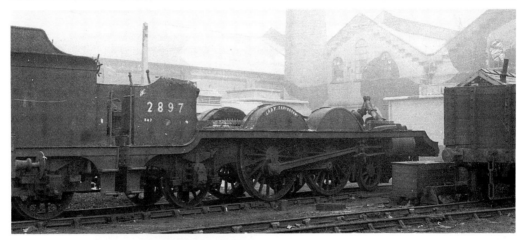

(top & centre) Two views of former GC Atlantic 2897 LADY FARINGDON which had been withdrawn in December 1947 and was on the 11th March 1948 being cut up at Gorton's scrapping annexe situated at the former Dukinfield Carriage & Wagon works. Other exGC locos resident on this day were 1347, 1349, 1478, 1484, 1486, 1492, 1498, 1678, 2920 and 2924. H.C.Casserley.

In its last few years of operation Gorton cut-up 70% of the locomotives entering the works, the remainder were repaired; however one was actually restored for preservation which I believe was a first, and last, for Gorton. D11 62660 BUTLER HENDERSON was repaired and repainted in the livery of the Great Central Railway and given its former GC number 506. It was eventually handed over to the BTC and is now part of the National Collection. Here it languishes in one of the Gorton shops, in 1962, resplendent in its 'new' paintwork. Authors collection.

HORWICH

Horwich Works was established by the Lancashire & Yorkshire Railway in 1887 for the manufacture and repair of locomotives. The green field site was in a rather exposed position and for those who ever visited the place in the cooler months of the year memories of the prevailing winds will come to mind. Locomotive building at Horwich was carried on until the early 1960's when the last of the BR 350 h.p. diesel-electric shunters were turned out. The types of steam locomotive built over the years ranged from the many L&Y types, through various LMS standard classes and latterly BR Standard types. Ranging in size from 2-8-0 tender engines to 0-4-0 tank engines, the works were responsible for building more than 2,000 locomotives in all. As late as 1953 Horwich got an order for five 0-4-0 Dock saddletanks based on a 1930's LMS design built by an outside contractor and which had cost £1,500 each in 1932; the price some 21 years later was £7,750 each.

Locomotive repairs accounted for most of the work carried out at Horwich and it has been estimated that over 50,000 steam locomotives were repaired there over the years. Although the majority of engines repaired were of ex-L&Y origin, former LNWR types could be seen receiving attention during the 1920's and 30's. LMS standard types accounted for many repairs in the 1950's and 60's and it was Stanier 8F No.48756 which had the distinction of being the last steam locomotive repaired by Horwich, that event in May 1964 saw the Works concentrating its efforts on maintaining electric multiple units, wagons and containers. Horwich locos were amongst the last pre-group types to see service on BR, the reliable 'A' class lasting until the 1960s.

In 1987, virtually 100 years after opening, the last vestiges of railway work, the iron foundry, was sold off to a private concern.

Many of the Horwich 'shops' are still standing today and a glimpse, across the valley from the M61 motorway, of the long former erecting shop building is a stark reminder of how great our railways once were and how much heavy engineering capacity this country once possessed and is probably lost forever.

Horwich erecting shop in 1925 with the last two of the ten Hughes 'Baltic' tanks virtually complete. These locomotives, weighing in at nearly 100 tons, were the heaviest tank engines ever to run in Britain and had but a short life of less than twenty years. No.11118 is being swung over to the centre road of the shop by the two 50 tons capacity overhead cranes installed that year. From the centre road the loco will begin its journey to the Paint Shop where, for some three more weeks it will be scoured, filled, rubbed down, leaded, painted and varnished before hand-over to the Operating Department. It was the intention of the Lancashire & Yorkshire Railway to produce a further twenty of these huge tank engines but in the event twenty more 4-6-0 tender engines, on which the design was based, were built instead. The LMS authorities at the time required more main line passenger tender engines for long distance work, off the Central Division, rather than another batch of what essentially were only medium distance passenger engines designed for the short but heavy workings of that division. Behind 11118 is one of the first of the more successful Hughes 2-6-0 mixed traffic engines known to most as 'Crabs' or Horwich 'Moguls'. Authors collection.

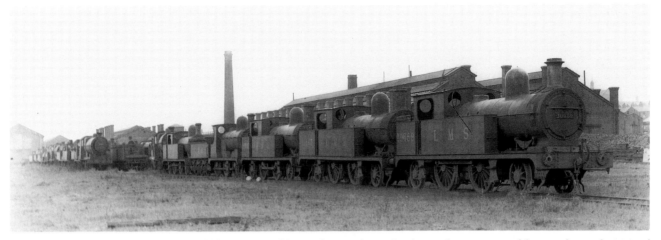

'The Farm' on the eve of war 11th June 1939. This area of the works was situated at the south-east corner of the complex, and was used to store redundant locomotives prior to scrapping. 10659, the first in the long line of engines here, had been withdrawn during the previous November but, like most of the others with it, was not cut-up until about 1941. W.L.Good.

52831 was one of eleven Hughes 6F 0-8-0's (L&Y Class Q3) to survive into BR days and is seen here awaiting scrapping after withdrawal from Wigan (L&Y) shed in 1951. The once sixty-nine strong class, built mainly during the Great War, included a number of rebuilds from L&Y Class Q1. Here on 'The Farm' scrapping had started in earnest by the 1950's and was not to let-up until 1964 when steam locomotives were no longer dealt with at Horwich. W.Potter.

One of the resident Works Shunters, still wearing its LMS number 11305, maintains a head of steam on Sunday 9th August 1953. These saddletanks originated from 0-6-0 goods tender engines built 1876-87 to a Barton Wright design but were rebuilt by Aspinall in the 1890's. Of the original 230 rebuilt all made it to Grouping and the last ones, amongst them the Horwich Works Shunters were not withdrawn until 1964. Notice the numerous D-ring shackles on the running plate, always handy for pulling those awkward items and, the extra long buffer shanks are worth a mention as is the 3-link coupling hanging below rail level.

Horwich was responsible for building 1,830 steam locomotives from 1889 to 1957. Its first was a 2-4-2 Radial tank No.1008 and the last, a BR Standard Class 4 2-6-0 No.76099. During that period the building of steam locomotives never let up except for the early years of World War Two when munitions production took over most of the works manufacturing capacity. Even after 76099 had left, locomotive building continued with 169 of the ubiquitous BR 0-6-0 diesel-electric shunters being erected up to December 1962. Ivatt Class 4 2-6-0 M3003 was one of the many LMS designs built here and came out of the erecting shop in 1948 carrying this M prefix. Here on 30th July 1950 the loco has returned for 'shopping' and will appear afterwards with the 'M' changed to a 4. W.Potter.

(centre) Seventy of the Horwich 'Moguls' were built there between 1926 and 1930 with the rest of the class built at Crewe. 2890 was one of a Crewe batch from 1930 and is seen at Horwich after a 'general' on 25th July 1937. W.L.Good.

(below) During 1925/26 twenty of the Compound 4-4-0 engines of Midland Railway origin were built at Horwich (1115-1134) and many were afterwards repaired there right up to the 1950's. 1101 had just completed a 'general' in February 1937 and is resplendent in crimson lake, the last time it would receive that livery. W.L.Good.

Besides the former L&YR and LMS standard locomotives maintained by Horwich, the works was also responsible for ex Furness Railway motive power and the occasional L&NWR engine. In July 1937 an ex-Furness 3F 0-6-0 No.12501 undergoes an 'intermediate' repair. W.L.Good.

This 'A' Class 0-6-0 had to be included not just because this class of engines comprised the most numerous of all the L&Y locomotives but also because they were for many the essence of the L&Y. The last examples were working until 1961 and during the LMS period were sent far and wide where in most cases they were accepted for what they were, solid very and dependable workhorses. 52338 stands alongside the south wall of the erecting shop in June 1957 awaiting attention. A.G.Ellis.

One of Bolton's Steam Rail Motors No.10609, looking a bit ragged, waits to enter the erecting shop in July 1937. The assemblage was one of eighteen introduced by Hughes between 1906 and 1911 for working branch lines such as Blackrod - Horwich and Sowerby Bridge - Rishworth amongst others. The first one had been withdrawn in 1927 and the last one just made it into BR ownership. W.L.Good.

The Ramsay Turbo-Electric Condensing locomotive on one of the Paint Shop roads at Horwich in 1923. Built in 1921 by Armstrong, Whitworth & Co. Ltd at their Newcastle-on-Tyne plant, this unconventional locomotive was tested on various sections of the LMS during 1923. During the summer of that year it carried out test runs on the Central Division between Bolton and Horwich and between Horwich and Southport being stabled at Horwich Works between runs. The results of the tests were apparently quite encouraging but the 70 foot locomotive, weighing nearly 155 tons, with a 2-6-6-2 wheel arrangement was, like so many other innovations tried out on our railways, not accepted as a form of motive power and so was never taken on. Authors collection.

Aspinall 2-4-2T about 1931 in the LMS livery applied by Horwich at the time i.e. 18 inch numerals and 14 inch letters. The locomotive is standing by the open traverser doors of the erecting shop. B.Matthews.

HORWICH. Locomotives 'on works'
21st September 1952

LOCO	SHED	REPAIR
YARDS AND PAINT SHOP		
40121	6C	INT
42796	24A	GEN
42871	26A	GEN
42928	11E	GEN
42944	2B	GEN
42982	6B	INT
43006	12D	INT
44067	1C	GEN
44080	9F	TEN
44300	5E	GEN
44445	6H	INT
44595	5E	GEN
44729	27C	TEN
48123	20D	INT
48209	19C	GEN
48749	9D	GEN
49603	26B	GEN
49617	27B	WITH
49672	27B	GEN (a)
50622	20E	GEN (b)
50799	25B	WITH
51512	26B	INT
52037	25A	GEN (b)
52139	26A	INT
52239	26A	INT
52355	25E	INT
52357	27D	WITH
52416	27B	INT
52517	26A	GEN
52588	27B	WITH
WORKS SHUNTERS		
11305	—	—
11324	—	—
11368	—	—
11394	—	—
51429	—	—
ERECTING SHOP		
40076	2E	INT
40097	4D	INT
42708	26A	GEN
42715	26A	INT
42810	5B	GEN
42825	21A	GEN
42931	1A	GEN
42938	9A	N/C
42946	3D	INT
42968	5B	N/C
43004	12D	GEN
43039	20A	N/C
44060	11A	GEN
44220	27D	GEN
44280	10E	GEN
44349	9A	N/C
44360	3D	INT
44443	1C	INT
44507	5D	GEN
48083	19C	INT
48138	16C	INT
48157	20A	N/C
48167	18D	GEN
48213	18D	GEN
48221	18A	GEN
48386	15A	INT
48510	8A	GEN
48661	18B	N/C
48719	6C	INT
49637	27D	CAS

LOCO	SHED	REPAIR
50651	24B	INT
51358	25D	GEN
51439	8C	INT
51530	27B	INT
52093	27B	GEN
52108	20C	INT
52218	27B	GEN
52429	2D	INT
52464	27B	GEN
52494	12E	INT
76000	NEW	—
76001	NEW	—
76002	NEW	—

Total: **79**

Key:
CAS - Casual repair.
GEN - General repair.
INT - Intermediate repair.
N/C - Non-Classified.
WITH - Withdrawn.
(a) General repair and removal of ACFI equipment.
(b) In for General but withdrawn.

(below) WREN was one of the eight narrow gauge works shunters which served Horwich from 1887 to 1962. The engines pottered around, most usefully it might be said, the extensive 18 inch gauge system and in this undated photograph WREN is situated near to one of the five sheds provided to house the tiny 0-4-0's. To the right is the Spring Smithy shop and, in the background, the east end of the Erecting Shop. This particular locomotive is now preserved as part of the National Collection. Authors collection.

(bottom) WREN in March 1961 outside the erecting shop in the company of ZM 32 a four wheel diesel from Ruston, brought in to help out during the final years of steam locomotive repairs at Horwich. I.G.Holt.

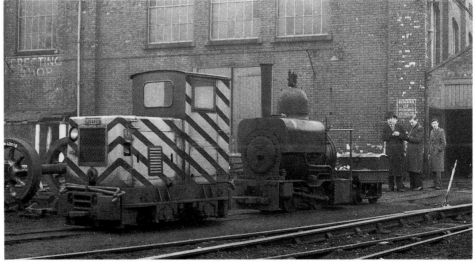

INVERURIE

Excepting the Lochgorm Works of the Highland Railway at Inverness, Inverurie was the most northerly of all the locomotive works inherited by British Railways. Opened in 1903 by the Great North of Scotland Railway, it replaced smaller premises at Kittybrewster in Aberdeen.

Not known for its locomotive building pedigree, with only ten locomotives built over a twelve year period up to 1921, Inverurie nevertheless provided a useful workshop in a far flung corner of the Kingdom. As usual, after Grouping, the Works provided repair facilities for the diminishing GNofSR locomotive fleet but as the LNER sent different pre-group and LNER built engines to replace them, Inverurie took on the 'shopping' of more diverse types. Probably the most famous of the larger engines to have regular repairs at Inverurie were the twenty five B12 4-6-0's of Great Eastern origin sent to the Northern Scottish Area of the LNER from 1931 onwards. Other types came and went, sometimes on a regular basis whilst others entered the 'shops' for a fleeting repair. More than any other of the main locomotive workshops of the LNER, Inverurie carried out the most minor of repairs for its motive power area whereas in areas further south those same repairs would have been usually performed at district level. In 1945 the LNER allocated certain classes to certain works and Inverurie was given charge of all or parts the following classes for repair: B12 (part); D31; D40; D41; D42; G10; J36 (part); J67 (part); J69 (part); Y9 (part); Z4; Z5. During the BR period even more diverse types appeared at Inverurie when engines of the former LMS, and its constituents, came for repair and scrapping.

The locomotive shops, though small, were well laid out and were adjacent to the Carriage & Wagon shops. In the early 1950's BR spent a considerable amount of money installing new overhead cranes in the erecting shop and generally refurbishing the whole place. In the latter part of that decade diesel locomotives came for repair and besides using the Erecting Shop, part of the old Carriage & Wagon shop, which had been modified, was utilised for the purpose; from the tiny 0-4-0 mechanical shunters to the large 135 ton English Electric Type 4's, any diesel locomotive working in the Scottish Region could be found there. After steam locomotives had all but disappeared from the north-east corner of Scotland, Inverurie continued to maintain diesel locomotives up to closure in 1969.

Locomotives cut up at Inverurie during the period 1961 to 1964 alone were many and varied; to list them all would be virtually impossible but a selection (BR numbers only are given) taken from official and unofficial sources gives an idea of the scale of the job and the types involved:

1961 - 40574, 40579, 40594, 40603, 40604, 40611, 40622, 40648, 40653, 40688, 43868, 43883, 43922, 54475, 54483, 54487, 54488, 54505, 55126, 55185, 55198, 55200, 55202, 55236, 56240, 56246, 56376, 57232, 57324, 57349, 57356, 57373, 57552, 57554, 57572, 57609, 61784, 62474, 62479, 62495, 62671, 62682, 62690, 64462, 64471, 64476, 64482, 64489, 64493, 64494, 64504, 64512, 64524, 64534, 64539, 64565, 64576, 64596, 64636, 64707, 64815, 64916, 65227, 65233, 65261, 65276, 65281, 65285, 65295, 65339, 68456, 68459, 68471, 69012, 69136, 69143, 69173, 69180, 69221.

1962 - 40614, 40618, 40619, 40645, 40647, 40650, 40663, 44008, 44016, 44253, 44254, 44258, 44319, 47168, 47536, 54482, 54491, 54493, 55165, 55207, 55208, 55215, 55216, 55220, 55222, 55226, 55227, 55229, 55230, 55232, 55233, 55261, 56305, 57233, 57246, 57257, 57331, 57378, 57411, 57429, 57445, 57557, 57559, 57560, 57585, 57613, 57671, 61968, 61996, 61998, 64461, 64471, 64480, 64500, 64533, 64542, 64545, 64553, 64566, 64578, 64590, 64598, 64604, 64607, 64628, 64630, 64637, 64794, 64963, 65232, 65246, 65266, 65280, 65296, 65313, 65318, 65330, 68338, 69137, 69204, 90513.

1963 - 43902, 44257, 45049, 57240, 57253, 57259, 57269, 57336, 57565, 57607, 57617, 57631, 57634, 57645, 60819, 60827, 60840, 60851, 60894, 60898, 60920, 60937, 60959, 60972, 61260, 64491, 64499, 64510, 64543, 64556, 64557, 64568, 64581, 64594, 64600, 64609, 64617, 64627, 64629, 64786, 64795, 64822, 64946, 64950, 64986, 65210, 65217, 65218, 65237, 65241, 65253, 65257, 65260, 65261, 65268, 65304, 65312, 65316, 65321, 65334, 65341, 65900, 65928, 67605, 67606, 67615, 67644, 67649, 67655, 67668, 67674, 68101, 68119, 68335, 68346, 68445, 68448, 68453, 68470, 68479, 69135, 69150, 69224, 90077, 90193, 90536, 90542, 90575.

1964 - 45465, 60089, 60098, 60159, 60161, 60162, 60804, 60838, 61117, 64562, 64579, 64583, 64591, 64593, 64603, 64619, 90058. Scrapping ceased.

The last steam locomotives were cut up in 1964 but diesel locomotives were occasionally dealt with up to closure of the works.

Before entering the Erecting Shop for dismantling, all engines were given a thorough clean with high pressure hot water. This unidentified ex-LMS 2P 4-4-0 was one of many of its type to visit Inverurie for repair in the 1950's; many were also cut-up here. M.Rayner.

(opposite) Slung beneath the new 100 ton capacity crane J37 no.64569 is taken to its repair bay in the Erecting Shop on 19th August 1955. The new crane could work independently and, equipped with two 50 ton hoists and two 10 ton auxiliary hoists, only one operator was required whereas in other workshops with less modern equipment two cranes, working in tandem, would be required to lift a locomotive. J35 no.64533 is receiving a 'heavy intermediate' and would be returned to traffic on the 25th. BR.

A postcard view of the Inverurie complex nestling in probably the most picturesque railway workshop location in Britain. The long white building in the centre is the C&W shops with the locomotive shops to the left. Authors collection.

(above) Detail of the underside of 64569 can be clearly seen in this view. British Railways.

(left) B12 no.1508 alongside the Erecting Shop at some unknown date in late 1946. These 4-6-0's became the staple motive power for passenger traffic in this part of Scotland and most ended their days at Inverurie. J.Robertson.

(above) The tender of 64569 was dealt with in another section of the Erecting Shop and is seen slung under the new 40 ton capacity crane en route to its repair bay. Other engines are in various stages of repair, the nearest showing how thorough the 'general' class of repair was. British Railways.

(right) J36 no.65224 has its left-hand frame drilled during a 'heavy intermediate' repair in June 1955. Notice the D-shackle on the mobile drilling machine; this enabled the heavy rig to be moved around the shop by the overhead crane. British Railways.

This J37, standing outside the south end of the Erecting Shop on 29th August 1956, has just completed a 'general' (it entered works 19/7/56) and steam is being raised ready for its return to its home shed in Edinburgh. L.R.Peters.

Ex-NER G5 no.67287 arrived in Scotland (as LNER 1889) in March 1943 with sister engine 1914 (BR 67292) and was sent to Keith for pilot duties and to work the Banff branch. 67287 eventually ended up at Kittybrewster and from there was employed as Inverurie Works Pilot where in June 1952 she was captured on film in the works yard going about her business. In March of the following year 67287 was withdrawn and cut-up at the works. Alec Swain.

(above) The south end of the works yard on 21st August 1947 contained this motley collection awaiting scrapping. D40 no.2280, with its SOUTHESK nameplate still attached, had been withdrawn in the previous January. Ten of the twenty one locomotives of this class were built at Inverurie between April 1909 and September 1921, the others were built by Neilson Reid & Co. (5), and North British Loco. Co. (6), 2280 (as G.N.S.R. 54) being the last one of those six in October 1920. The tenders all still carry the wartime N.E. identification. D.A.Dant.

(centre) At lunchtime on Wednesday 8th April 1953 this was all that was left of D41 no.62241 as the scrapping crew take their break. Withdrawn in February, the engine had latterly worked from Keith shed. L.R.Peters.

(right) On the same day in another part of the Inverurie scrapyard was this former Caledonian 0-4-4 tank. Withdrawn the previous November, cutting up was completed in June. Former LMS engines had started to arrive at Inverurie for repair in 1949 and continued to do so until 1964. When the former Glasgow & South Western Railway works at Kilmarnock ceased to function as a scrapyard in 1959 many more former CR locomotives came to Inverurie for scrapping. By 1964 BR was selling most of its redundant locomotives to private scrapyards and one of the less glorious functions of this Scottish locomotive works was finished. L.R.Peters.

STRATFORD

Stratford Works comprised two locomotive workshops separated by a main line, a carriage works and the engine shed. Both dated from Great Eastern days and the oldest, opened in 1847, was situated on the east (Up) side of the Cambridge line, adjacent to Stratford station and was built at a right angle to that line. Locomotive access to the old works was via a turntable which could fit a medium sized 4-6-0 (B12), without its tender, the latter dealt with in another shop, across the main lines, near the Paint Shop. The more modern workshop, built on land known as High Meads, was erected in 1915 and had rail access at both ends of the two adjoining erecting shops that comprised the building.

Stratford had started to build locomotives from 1850 but up to the mid 1880's the GER still relied on outside contractors to supply many of its locomotives. The appointment of James Holden as Locomotive Superintendent in 1885 saw Stratford become one of the most efficient and self contained locomotive works, for its size, in the country and turning out the majority of the GE motive power. By 1899 it was turning out its 1,000th locomotive and the trend on self reliance was continued by Holden's son and later by A.J.Hill who was responsible for the additional facility at High Meads.

Because of weight restrictions abounding on its railway, the Great Eastern was forced to build locomotives of smaller stature than those found on many other lines but nevertheless some superb, powerful and no less handsome classes emerged from Stratford shops and many went on to serve not only the LNER but also British Railways. After 1924 no more locomotives were built at Stratford and the two workshops concentrated on repairs. By 1947 no less than thirty six separate classes of LNER steam locomotive had regular repairs at Stratford and by the early fifties other 'foriegn' engines started to appear; diesel shunters and BR Standards also came in for repair. In the last six years of steam repair at Stratford the scrapping of redundant steam locomotives was stepped up and hundreds were eventually cut-up there with some surprising entrants to the scrapyard.

6th August 1954. The following were undergoing repair on the Old Works: 43064 **H/I**, 61538 **G**, 62523 **G**, 62566 **G**, 62572 **G**, 64641 **G**, 64650 **G**, 64653 **G**, 64689, 64708 **G**, 64807 **C/L**, 64970 **G**, 65438 **C/L**, 65445 **G**, 65570 **G**, 65572 **C/L**, 67201 **G**, 67230 **G**, 69574 **G**, 69650 **C/L**, 69651 **G**, 69725 **G**.

New Works: 43058 **H/I**, 43149 **H/I**, 61119 **G**, 61335 **G**, 61364 **G**, 61514 **G**, 61547 **G**, 61557 **G**, 61576 **G**, 61579 **G**, 61614 **G**, 61617 **G**, 62526 **G**, 62582 **G**, 64681 **G**, 64768 **G**, 64826 **G**, 64976 **G**, 64984 **G**, 64987 **G**, 65508 **G**, 65532 **G**, 65589 **G**, 68494 **G**.

Outside High Meads is one of Stratford's own, Super Claud 8839 after rebuilding in 1928 to Class D16/2. Turned out by the Great Eastern in July 1908 as a saturated engine (GER no.1839, Class D56), its was superheated in 1922 and at Grouping became LNER Class D15. The 1928 rebuilding saw the engine getting an extended smokebox which certainly enhanced its looks even more. The 121 Clauds which comprised LNER classes D14, D15 and D16 were built during the period 1900 to 1923, the first 111 had appeared by 1911 but the last ten not until after Grouping. After various rebuilding and upgrading most entered service with British Railways and the last example, 62613, was not scrapped until 1960. They were the essence of the Great Eastern and sadly none were preserved but at least the works that built them also scrapped all of them. Authors collection.

Looking towards the west end of High Meads Erecting Shop on 10th March 1955 from one of the overhead cranes. This building contained two erecting shops, the north shop is just out of picture to the right, with a machine shop in between. On the right hand road of this shop, N2 69492, of King's Cross, is a new arrival and has come in for a 'casual light' repair. The centre road contains 61223, one of the Cambridge B1's which had come to Stratford on the 24th January for a 'general' and on this date still has another week in shops before being released to traffic. On the left hand road are L1's nos.67716, 67753 and 67751; all are extremely grimy and in for tank and bunker welding; 'general'; 'casual light' repairs respectively. At the end of 1957 the High Meads building was closed for steam locomotive repairs and the whole place was refurbished for diesel maintenance although the 40 ton capacity overhead cranes, still only forty years old, were retained. British Railways.

On the same day another B1, 61329 of Stratford, is married to its wheels at the completion of a 'general' during which it had received a refurbished boiler (no.28841). Within three days, after a touch of paint where necessary and a new set of cab numbers, the B1 was back with the Running Department for another two years before its next general overhaul at Stratford. Hiding behind the B1 is N7 no.69709 which was in for a 'light' repair. British Railways.

(left) This Claud was in the shops for a 'general' in February 1956 and on the 5th of that month was stuck outside in the rain whilst its boiler was being repaired. Notice the temporary buffer block attached to the left side of the drag box to prevent any damage whilst being shunted. 62511 went back to traffic on the 3rd March. L.R.Peters.

The erecting shop in the old works functioned until 1963 when it was closed down under the BR workshops rationalisation scheme. This view dates from the May of 1947 but could have been any time from 1920 to 1960. British Railways.

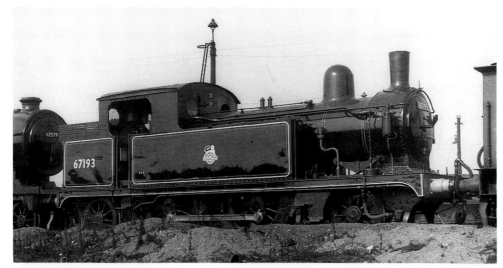

This was how Stratford turned out its charges in 1953. After completing a 'general' F5 no.67193 stands out in the March sunshine resplendent in its black lined paintwork. A.R.Goult.

(centre) One of the nice things about the Stratford complex, and complex it definitely was, would be the variety of the motive power to be found about the place. In July 1948 this tiny, slightly undressed, Y7 had just arrived from Tyne Dock having been withdrawn the previous month from North Eastern Region operating stock but then given a new lease of life to become one of Stratford's works shunters. 8088 was a relatively young member of the Y7 class, the oldest were built at Gateshead in 1888 and the last ones, 8088 included, emerged from Darlington in 1923 from whence it went to work on the dock lines in Hull. Many of the robust little engines were sold off to private industry and after its spell at Stratford, in Departmental Stock as 68088, this example was sold to the National Coal Board in October 1952 and in a happy ending to a nomadic career it was purchased in 1964 for preservation and is now to be found at Loughborough. L.R.Peters.

(left) When the Metropolitan Railway steam locomotive fleet was sold to the LNER in 1937 responsibility for their maintenance fell on Stratford and in April 1947 Class L2 no.9071 was to be found alongside High Meads waiting to enter the shops for a 'light' repair. The L2 did not return to traffic until 16th August! L.R.Peters.

As already mentioned, Stratford Works had its own dedicated fleet of tank engines and this Y4, dating from 1921, spent its entire working life at the locomotive shops of the old works until they closed in 1963. Numbered Departmental 33 from 1952, the Y4 had been specifically built to run over the sharp curves found inside the 'old works' yards. Four other Y4's had also been built to work local goods yards where six coupled engines were barred. Authors collection.

J92 Crane Tank 68669 was one of three such engines employed at Stratford and it is seen here on the Works engine shed yard in September 1950, "stopped". During the following month it was withdrawn so had probably never recovered from its status here. None of the cranes attached to the engines had worked since before Grouping and the chains and hooks were removed at some unknown date. A.R.Goult.

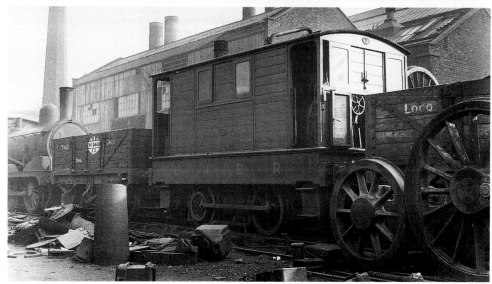

Y6 no. 7132 and J15 no. 7694 on the scrap line, situated between the Stripping Shed and the Iron Foundry, in October 1931 surrounded by remnants of previous occupants. The tram engine was, up to 1927, one of the passenger engines used on the Wisbech and Upwell railway and had emerged from Stratford in 1883. Locofotos

SWINDON

Centre of an empire - the vast sprawling complex of the Great Western Railway facility at Swindon employed some 8,000 people by 1948 of which 3,800 worked in the locomotive works. Of all the railway companies the GWR was the only one that had survived without any real infighting, reorganisation and managerial changes; basically it had, before 1948, over a century of "getting on with the job" under its belt.

This confidence was mirrored in its Locomotive Department which throughout the 20th century had produced better engines with each new design, falling back on experience and prior knowledge. The works at Swindon were geared up to produce quality and when necessary quantity. The opening of 'A' shop in 1902 was again a sign of confidence; its vast hall housing dozens of locomotives each designated to its own repair or building bay. Some of the illustrations herein give a good idea of the size of 'A' shop and anybody who visited Swindon will remember the lasting impression the place gave as one entered unable at first to take it all in. Although Swindon was renowned for producing quality it was also known for sticking to tradition. When the British Railways Modernisation Plan was announced Swindon already had ideas of its own about what form of motive power would replace steam. So main line diesel-hydraulic traction was introduced to Britain via Swindon whilst the works was still producing steam locomotives in the shape of the BR 9F 2-10-0's. The rest of the story is well documented but the diesel-hydraulic era at Swindon spelled the end of locomotive building there for good except for a small export order in the early 1980's. Had Swindon upset the powers that be for sticking to traditionalism? Whatever, the works never recovered from the 1960's and the massive facility along with its skilled personnel were not required and Swindon Locomotive Works closed for good in 1986 marking the end of nearly 150 years of quality.

Swindon's 'A' Shop on the 25th February 1957 with new construction being carried out alongside repairs. In the left foreground can be seen the bogies of the gas-turbine locomotive 18000, its body elsewhere in the shop, and moving on, left to right, we next come to the first sections of the underframe of the initial 2,000 h.p. diesel-hydraulic Warship, D800. Alongside, the new boiler of 9F 92096 shares the same bay as the tender body for a new BR Standard Class 4, whilst 4090 DORCHESTER CASTLE, completing a 'general', occupies the next bay. On this day the vast 'A' Shop also housed the following locomotives: (steam) 1007, 1016, 1028, 1458, 2835, 2837, 2856, 3206, 3440, 3653, 3656, 3746, 3850, 4061, 4074, 4075, 4077, 4082, 4085, 4091, 4098, 4134, 4161, 4651, 4702, 4982, 4984, 5017, 5030, 5062, 5069, 5080, 5090, 5932, 5933, 5938, 5974, 6003, 6024, 6025, 6135, 6300, 6353, 6845, 6863, 6879, 6932, 6982, 6994, 7008, 7237, 7786, 7904, 7909, 7913, 7918, 8484, 8491, 8760, 9408, 9414, 46509, 70022, 70027, 75025, 78006, 82004, 92007; (diesel) 13102, 15100, 15107, 15231, 15235; (new construction) 75057, 75058, 75059, 75060 and 92096. Some thirty eight other locomotives were about the works on the same day. British Railways.

(right) New construction in October 1933 comprised, amongst others, this nearly complete 0-4-2 tank no.4820. In the same bay but out of picture to the right were 4821 and 4822. On the far side of the traverser avenue a 2-6-2T is made ready for lifting. Locofotos.

(centre) The south entrance to 'A' Shop, circa 1960, with 2-6-2T 4104 freshly emerged from a heavy repair. The traverser can be seen just inside the entrance. Authors collection.

(below) 6979 HELPERLY HALL and 7809 CHILDLEY MANOR share adjacent bays in 'A' Shop on 28th April 1963. Steam repairs were coming to an end although nearly two years would go by before they ceased completely. The last repair, excluding any for preservation purposes, was given to exLMS Ivatt Mogul No.43003 (see also Horwich) which left works during the second week of February 1965. With regard to the 4-6-0s, one wag suggested that HELPLESSLY HALL and TIDDLY MANOR would have been much more interesting names. D.Butterfield per N.E.Stead.

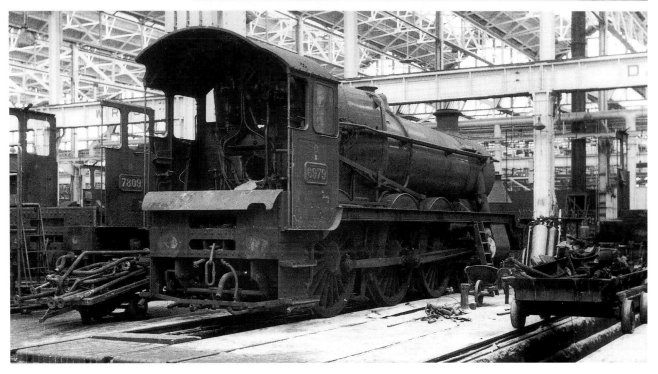

The Engine Pool, where engines due for 'shopping' and those ex-works congregated, was situated at the east end of the locomotive shops, in the fork of the junction of the Bristol and Gloucester lines. On the 5th October 1947 four ex-works engines, coupled together, straddle the throat waiting for the tow to Swindon shed whilst one of the Works Shunters hauls two dead engines off to the shops. The presence of so many tenders in this area of the works is explained by the fact that the camera is perched on the roof of the Tender Shop. Authors collection.

BR Standard Class 3 2-6-2T 82018 nears completion in August 1952 and was part of the first batch of ten (82010 - 82019) built for the Southern Region. Of the British Railways standard classes Swindon built all 45 of the BR Cl.3 tank engines also all the BR Cl.3 tender engines (77000 - 77019) and all 80 of the Cl.4 4-6-0's (75000 - 75079) but it will probably be best remembered for building the 53 Cl.9F 2-10-0's (92087 - 92096, 92178 - 92220) between September 1957 and March 1960 of which 92220 EVENING STAR was the last steam locomotive built for British Railways. L.R.Peters.

Two typically Swindon products 43XX class 2-6-0's 4305 and 6309 pose alongside 'A' Shop in 1931. Locofotos.

Being equipped with a locomotive testing plant, Swindon was often asked by other Regions to test certain classes so that recommendations could be made from the results. One such group of tests were conducted in 1949/50 on one of Blackpool's exLMS Ivatt Cl.2's no.46413. It was tested 'out on the road' and was, for the benefit of comparison, tried against a GW 0-6-0 Dean Goods and against which, before modifications, it did not do too well. A chimney extension was fitted by Swindon and in this view of 46413 in June 1950 the protrusion can be seen sticking out of the chimney top. Eventually the whole class was fitted with taller chimneys and the Ivatt Cl.2's turned out to be better engines for it. D.C.Riley.

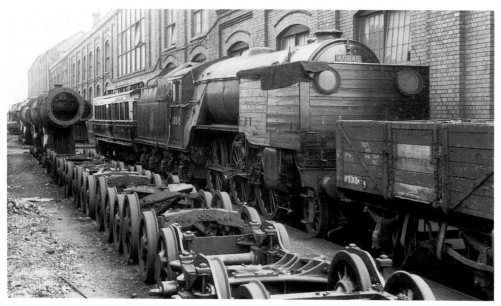

Another 'foreigner' in for testing was V2 60845 and in this view of 22nd February 1953 at Swindon, the Eastern Region engine is fitted with an indicator shelter for road testing. This was not the first time the V2 had come for testing, its previous visit had lasted only for a few months during the summer of 1952 but in late October it returned to carry out further testing, the result of which saw twenty V2's having their draughting altered. L.R.Peters collection.

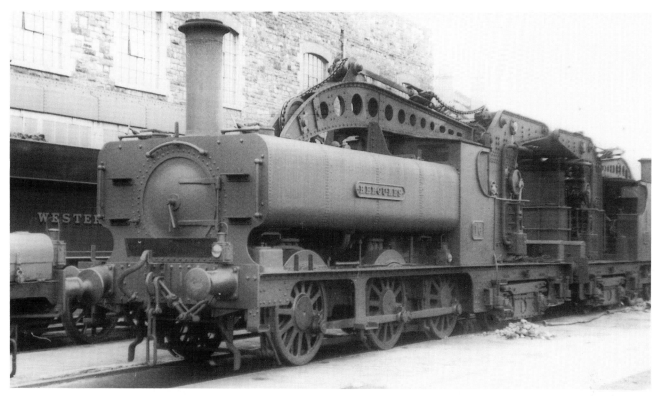

The Great Western had three of these crane tanks as works shunters up to 1936 and no.16 HERCULES is stabled back to back with no.18 STEROPES over the weekend of 25th and 26th April 1931. The other crane tank was no.17 CYCLOPS (based at Wolverhampton Works) which, with no.18, had been built in 1901 whilst no.16 was the youngest of the trio by some twenty years. All were classified as 0-6-4T Crane and were withdrawn in 1936. Other crane tanks found at Swindon included an ex South Devon Railway 2-4-0T no.1299 rebuilt as a crane tank for shunting duties at the works. The last steam locomotives at the works were in fact those employed on internal shunting duties (8405, 9425 and 9457) up to the end of 1965. W.L.Good.

Scenes of Swindon scrapyard shortly after the broad gauge was abolished are well known but views showing activity in the 1930's are not so well recorded. However this 1931 photograph is more akin to the private breakers yards of the 1960's with engine parts strewn all over the place. Being broken-up are 3816 COUNTY OF LEICESTER and 3809 COUNTY WEXFORD both, it will be noted, still fitted with name and number plates. Locofotos.

(above & opposite) Two views of 'A' Shop in December 1959 with steam locomotive repairs still in full swing alongside the new construction of Warship diesel hydraulics. Identifiable steam locomotives are 5024 *CAREW CASTLE* and 6006 *KING GEORGE I*. The diesels being built are in the number range D817 to D826. D804 had come in for modifications to its roof. The construction of the first 'Warships' presented something of a problem for the Swindon workforce and when D800 was being built most of the bodywork was constructed without the aid of jigs. It was from D800 that all the formers and jigs were fashioned and fabricated and construction of the rest of the class was eventually speeded up so that they were being turned out at the rate of one every three weeks. At this time, in another section of 'A' Shop, the last steam locomotives built for BR were being assembled. Authors collection.

By November 1963 the diesels had virtually taken over the west side of 'A' Shop as this line of Warships and Westerns shows and only one steam locomotive, a BR Std. Cl.5. resides. However there are still plenty of steam locomotives on the other side of the shop and more diverse classes, not normally associated with Swindon, were arriving for repair each week such as exLMS Moguls of the Stanier and Ivatt variety. New construction, in the foreground, comprised the 650 h.p. Diesel Hydraulic 0-6-0's of the D9500 class; the last locomotives built by Swindon for BR. E.Bradley.

In connection with the naming of 92220 EVENING STAR, on the 18th March 1960, an exhibition was held showing the latest Swindon locomotives and rolling stock. This is the view inside the shop just a few days prior to the naming ceremony when Warship D818 GLORY was being finished off to take part. Behind on its plinth is NORTH STAR with two fitters posing for the camera. E.Bradley.

Outside 'A' Shop on the same day A.E.C. railcar No.4, restored to full GWR brown and cream livery and lettered Great Western, heads a line of 'latest product' railcars which were, front to rear, Trans-Pennine trailer car E59765 and 3-car cross-country set W50689, W50754 and W59297. Warship D817 stands alongside. E.Bradley.

2069, the last pre-group 0-6-0 pannier tank to be withdrawn, travelled from Birkenhead to Swindon during April 1959 and is seen on the 3rd May in 'C' Shop awaiting its fate. It seems difficult to understand the reasoning behind such expenditure as sending the 0-6-0T on a 200 mile journey for scrapping when on the way it would virtually pass two former Great Western locomotive works (Oswestry and Wolverhampton) that were active in such fields. L.R.Peters.

More V2's at Swindon but this time for the attention of the cutters. This melancholy line-up on The Dump on 27th September 1964 included nine of the 2-6-2's: 60809, 60812, 60887, 60916, 60922, 60932, 60941, 60945, 60964, all minus tenders which had been taken away for conversion to snow ploughs. Other V2's in the same section were 60856 and 60975 whilst being cut-up in 'C' Shop were 60833 and 60925. The presence of these engines at Swindon for scrapping was part of the madness of the period when anything appeared to go anywhere just so long as it disappeared from sight. L.R.Peters.

WOLVERHAMPTON

Wolverhampton Stafford Road Works was the most modern of all the Great Western locomotive shops, new erecting shops being opened there as late as 1932. Previous to this development (enabled by the Government Loans & Guarantees Act of 1929), the old works at Wolverhampton had struggled on in cramped confinement, situated as it was between the Shrewsbury - Wolverhampton line and physically split in half by Stafford Road.

Many locomotives were built at the old works but by the time that the new shops were opened all new locomotive construction on the GWR was centred on Swindon workshops. Even the new premises were not blessed with an abundance of land area and in order to have the necessary freedom of movement for engines and tenders, three traversers were built into the site. With the opening of the new erecting shop, the old erecting shop on the east side of Stafford Road was abandoned and turned over to the Running department. The portion of works on the west side of Stafford Road, but divided from the new facilities by the line to Victoria Basin, was kept operable as this section contained the boiler shop, forge and smiths.

All sorts of standard GW classes came to Wolverhampton for repair although most of the large 4-6-0 passenger engines were 'shopped' at Swindon. Nevertheless many interesting and ancient locomotives graced the erecting shop when, for instance, the ex Cambrian works at Oswestry handed over 'general' repairs of its former charges to Wolverhampton. At its height Stafford Road employed over 600 personnel that were capable of performing the heaviest of repairs.

A visit to the works on Sunday 19th August 1962 noted the following: 1020, 1630, 3615, 3721, 4636, 4697, 4703, 5181, 5184, 5564, 6156, 6160, 6614, 6618, 7739, 7816, 8104, 9422, 9470, 9613, 9624, 9626, 9647, 9665, 82008. Waiting to enter works were: 3217, 4938, 4961, 5065, 5658, 7002, 7824, 9415. Notice the predominance of tank engines amongst the list also, by this date, certain of the large passenger engines had started to be 'shopped' at Wolverhampton rather than Swindon where steam repair was slowly being run down in favour of diesel locomotive repairs. The latter motive power, although at one time designated to be repaired at Stafford Road, never did enter the shops in any great numbers, if at all, and in February 1964 the last locomotive repair (2-8-0 No.2859 being that loco) was completed.

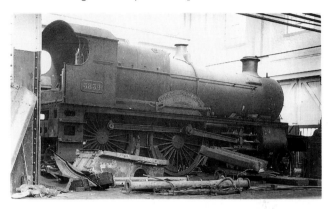

Old-timer 3834 COUNTY OF SOMERSET takes advantage of the facilities offered by the newly opened erecting shop in April 1932. H.C.Casserley.

(below) The western bay of the Erecting Shop in June 1950 with 6600 and 6418 under repair. Each of the two erecting bays was served by two 50 ton capacity overhead travelling cranes. Locofotos.

A Sunday visit during March 1960 finds a predominance of tank engines in the western bay of the erecting shop with 8792 and 3653 amongst them Notice the obligatory gaberdine, collar and tie attire of the period; unfortunately swept away by the anorak. W.Potter.

Enthusiasts roam the erecting shop on Sunday 14th June 1953. The only sounds heard in the place would be footsteps, the occasional gasp and the groan and hiss of heating pipes. During weekdays the noise at times was so bad that shouting was usually the only way to converse. W.Potter.

5188 stripped down to its bare essentials during a heavy repair in June 1953. W.Potter.

The yard, situated at the north end of the works, in May 1958. In the centre are locos awaiting 'shops', heading the lines are a 'Manor', a 66XX 0-6-2T and a 73XX 2-6-0. The building on the left was the weighhouse whilst that on the right was used to inspect engines prior to entry into the erecting shop. W.Potter.

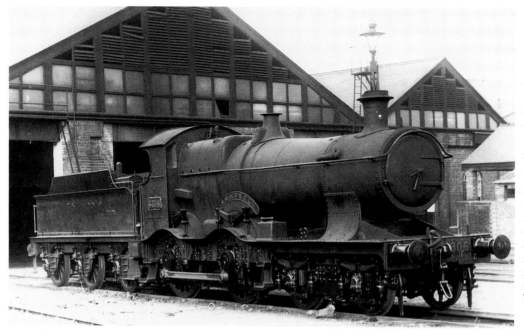

Prior to the commissioning of the new erecting shops locomotives arriving at Stafford Road for 'shopping' would be parked in the south yard of the engine shed. Similarly once repairs were complete engines would end up in the same place before returning to their home depots. 3306 ARMOREL stands outside one of the roundhouse sheds after receiving attention for collision damage in 1930. W.L.Good.

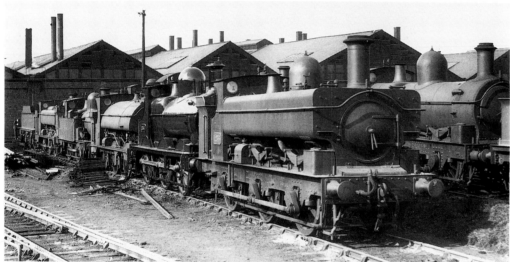

The works line-up outside the roundhouses in April 1932 with, from front to rear, 1253, ex-works 2551, 2107, 973 and 2120. H.C.Casserley.

973 appears to be the worse for wear as it awaits 'shopping' on 24th April 1932. H.C.Casserley.